The Beatitudes
in
Modern Life

THE BEATITUDES
in
MODERN LIFE

edited by Margaret Garvey

THE THOMAS MORE PRESS
Chicago, Illinois

ISBN 0-88347-219-8

Contents

Introduction

"Indeed in our age they talk about the importance of presenting Christianity simply, not elaborately and grandeloquently. And about this subject they write books, it becomes a science...but they forget or ignore the fact that the truly simple way of Christianity is to do it."

Kierkegaard
For Self Examination

W HEN approached about editing this book, I thought about a game I used to play with a friend on long drives. In the game we would construct the ideal dinner party. A dinner where friends and people we'd never met, but who had changed our lives through their examples and their written word, would join at table to enjoy a splendid meal. The eight writers I've asked to contribute to a *The Beatitudes in Modern Life* would be a splendid group for that ideal supper.

I've lived within the shadow of Notre Dame du lac, for six years. The University is a mile from my home. As a result, on any given evening, my husband and

Margaret Garvey

I host friends and people who are floating through the University. We indulge in food and wine and argument—usually about the Church. Often the theological arguments go over my head. I'm more of an "experiential learner." Most often though I want these academic friends to meet the "doers" that I've been privileged to meet: the Dorothy Days, the Jean Vaniers, the Dom Helder Camaras. I want them to meet the people whose sacrifice is their daily grind: the woman who has picketed our local abortion clinic faithfully every Friday morning for five years; the mother who is caring for her severely handicapped daughter rather than submit her to a state institution; the Cambodian woman who meets every plane carrying newly arrived Southeast Asian refugees in order to offer them hospitality. I'd love to have this come true.

Many evenings at our table I think that Peter Maurin, co-founder of the Catholic Worker, was not wrong when he wrote: "The scholars must collaborate with the workers in making a path from the things as they are to the things as they should be. The scholars must become workers so the workers may become scholars."

The eight contributors to this book are both workers and scholars and I am grateful for their lives. Each of them seems to embody the personalism called for in the Beatitudes. Each takes the Beatitudes as the root of the gospel message and presents us with radical options for change in our lives.

Introduction

Frank Sheed, in his book *To Know Christ,* speaks to the meaning of the beatitudes for this modern Church of ours: "It is a remarkable way of life, or program of life here sketched. Most of these things had been spoken of and right endurance of them praised in the Old Testament, but they had hardly been described as adding up to blessedness, a kind of fundamental bliss so that one would be dismissed by not having them. Mercy and cleanness of heart, yes. But sorrow and persecution and reviling and slander? Jesus is uncompromising about these."

These beatitudes aren't a "theological argument," they aren't ethereal; they speak to each of us and to the society in which we live. They seem to be Jesus' "inauguration speech" setting forward drastic changes we must make in our hearts in order to enter the Kingdom. They are not religious pop but blessings we are called to live. Simon Tugwell says about the Beatitudes, "they obviously call us to a tremendous height of spiritual and ethical achievement, yet at the same time they seem almost to canonize qualities which are the antithesis of achievement and success." What other kind of demand can we expect from a Son of God whose life began in a stable and ended in nudity on a cross?

Margaret Garvey

9

Blessed Are...

The Poor in Spirit

Brian Miclot

MOST of us would like to believe that the poor in spirit whom Jesus blessed were those who could renounce, those who could be detached, or those who could have possessions and take them or leave them. Especially in a land of considerable means, surely we can believe that nowadays even poverty is inflated. We adjust it and pro-rate it so that the possession of at least moderate means does not exclude possession of the kingdom. We can *have*, and live as if we *had not*. We can be hospitable, we can be generous, we can be with and act as if we were without. After all, isn't renunciation the acid test of real Christianity?

Renunciation *is* attested in the scriptures. Zebedee's sons leave behind their possessions, their trade and even their father to follow Jesus. Sent out, though, they do have something—not much, a walking stick, perhaps—but they do *have* something. At certain points, it seems as though Jesus is indifferent about the amount of possessions; the question rather seems to be detachment and stress management:

13

Brian Miclot

...do not worry about your livelihood, what you are to eat or drink or use for clothing. Is not life more than food? Is not the body more valuable than clothing? (Mt 6:25).

Following Jesus, the post-resurrection community held all things in common, but *hold* they did. And *holding on*, we have been doing ever since.

We would like to believe, therefore, that it is a question of attitude. And the answer is renunciation, detachment. We ask ourselves purging questions: Can we live as if the Lord could ask it of us tonight, and we could give it? Whatever it is, whatever possesses us most out of our possessions, whatever keeps us from following: could we give it up if the Lord asked? The "it" is that which we possess dearly, hold onto compulsively, or perhaps that which we couldn't see ourselves living without. We even purge further, remembering Abraham cherishing his son Isaac whom he was commanded to let go, or Jesus wanting his cup of suffering to pass. These were not like VCR's, or "the car & house," or any "pieces of the rock" to which our "Linus blanket" era holds tightly. These were dear: flesh and blood, health, the future and life itself. Following Jesus, we purge further.

We up the ante. We renounce not only things, but also kin and life itself. Would we be the same persons, we ask, would we have the same humanity or be our same selves with or without wealth of any kind? Things

The Poor In Spirit

aren't bad, and poverty's not that great. We could have things and still pass the test, we tell ourselves, if only we renounce.

Tom

But the poor of Luke's beatitudes are not just "good renouncers." They are poor. Period. The kingdom which Jesus preached and lived for and died for belongs to them. The kingdom belongs to people like Tom.

Like many of our urban elderly poor, Tom hung out at a tavern. Among other things, the tavern was his place for "the cure," a place for afternoon comradery and the space in which to be happy for a few hours. The tavern was where I met him. I was introduced to him by his friend Rick, who whispered to the side, "He drinks too much." Tom, at 67, was couched on the barstool beside his girlfriend Doris. After introductions and a few hours of cheer, I told Tom I'd stop by his place some time. I was interested. I wanted to see.

In a few weeks, I went to see him. I stood on his front porch, and, after knocking a while, I noticed a young boy crisscrossing the terrace on a three-wheeler.

"Have you seen Tom around?" I called out with my hands cupped around my mouth, announcing my interest.

The racer yelled back, as if a harbinger on horseback.

"He got shot! Someone came with a gun; then the police came! Now, he's in jail!"

"Who's in jail? Tom?" my heart raced into frantic question.

"No, that man with the gun. They took him away," came the answer.

"Is Tom ok? Is he in the hospital or in there?" I asked, pointing to the ripped screen window.

The boy sped away, shouting over his shoulder, "I don't know, but he got shot. The man had a gun."

I stood there on the porch—puzzled, apprehensive and sad. The porch was worn to a slant. Torn screens, peeling paint and a rundown neighborhood told only of the poor's plight. And now, violence. Of course, I said to myself, I should expect to find it in this neighborhood. Violence is the bottom line of boredom and powerlessness. It is the release of rage. But why, why does it take its toll on the gentle? Why explode and break apart the lowly ones? Especially Tom.

Later, I discovered that a friend named Doug had come in through Tom's open door, liquored up, carrying his new gun. Like a cowboy busting open saloon doors, he shot wildly at Tom's kitchen ceiling and floor. A bullet had taken a chunk of Tom's middle finger before rifling a hole in the carpet. With luck, the random violence of bullets had not killed Tom; it merely began to eat away. My interest in Tom had become an engagement and a different way of seeing. For the violence

The Poor In Spirit

in Tom's neighborhood was seldom like the car-chasing, contract-killing of media entertainment. It was, rather, a sinking—a bit-by-bit gnawing-away of person and goods from which there seemed no way to climb out and escape. This is the violence pressed upon the contemporary poor—the other America with its invisible wasting away.

It bears repeating: the poor of Luke's beatitudes are poor. Period. They are not just "good renouncers." Like Tom, they know their "need for God" (in some translations, in place of "poor in spirit") because all other ways of getting even, of shooting back, and all other "empowerment resources" have proven empty. They are poor. They are the ones who have lost the power to fight. It is not that they *will* no longer fight; they *can* no longer fight. Even fighting to get to the top, even upward mobility, means nothing to them; those are the lies and the oppression which seduced and raped them long ago.

The mobility of the poor in spirit and those who know their need for God is not upward or downward. It is, rather, agility. It is horizontal. It is expanding—a developmental non-exclusion which groans and grows until it embraces. They make no pretense that God will bless their achievements, by gaining a little more through invested talents, or even by volunteering to "have less." Their personal space, like Tom's, moves outward. Tom's space seemed always empty enough, poor enough, for others. This is what Donna and some of her friends discovered.

Donna was a native American for whom, like most others, the American (caucasian) dream translated as enough liquor to make it 'til morning. She never heard Buffy Saint-Marie's words "Can't you see that their poverty's profiting you?"; she lived them. Pregnant at 23 with her fourth child and tossed away by her third husband, she landed one day on Tom's porch. She'd been in and out of shelters and missions, evicted from most for breaking the rules. Tom offered a place.

Now, Tom's kitchen floor is a remarkable work of art. Carpeted by the landlord to upgrade the place for government qualification, the floor resembles a well-used mechanic's pad. Cigarette burns, reminiscent of the post-Impressionists' pointalism, speckle the floor from the perimeter of the table legs to the walls. Gallons of beer, crumbs enough to stuff turkey after turkey, pounds of kitty-litter and, yes, the bullet-hole have found their way *into* the carpet. They give the "painting" an indescribable texture and a "Realist's" odor. The floor *is* the kitty-box. The "artists" are those who have graced Tom's "studio" with hours of conversation, seeking food or warmth or the Cubs' game on TV or just a friend. This artistic "school" boasts such greats as Rufus, who died on the porch after last summer's 95-degree "pit" barbeque, John, Doug, Dave (the only one in the eight-room apartment house with a telephone), and now, Donna.

The Poor In Spirit

I wasn't there when Donna came for the "days of her confinement," but Tom told me of it later. It was simple. And single-hearted. "I let her sleep on the bed. I slept on the kitchen floor. She needed a place to stay." On the kitchen floor! Most of us, if a bedbug were found on our sheets, would scream. But, sleeping on *that* kitchen floor?! Really! For Tom, though, the floor became his space to make space. The movement of the poor is expansive, agile. It is a developmental non-exclusion which makes room and embraces. Tom's room is poor; it is empty enough for others.

There is a danger for us when we link upward and downward mobility with pluses or minuses in God's book of blessings. It is a confusion between the seen and the unseen or an hypothesis of correlation with no warrant by faith. For the life of the spirit, it is dangerous, even lethal. It is the lie which the "gospel of wealth" propagandized at the beginning of the 20th century: I have wealth; thus, God must be blessing me. But this is the lie which Job's truth remedied long ago. "The *Lord* gives, the *Lord* takes away . . ." regardless of one's place on the ladder.

In the life of the spirit, upward and downward mobility are in God's hands; ours is the horizontal task. We open to embrace, then open again. Notice that arms stretched out horizontally can receive more rain and sun and other gifts of the sky than those that are closed. At the same time, arms outstretched balance and confirm the feet's grasp of the ground. It is the ballet's position for *real* strength and readiness. It is open and strong. Ascension by success ladders and bootstraps, on the other hand, builds Babel because it confuses the language of God in the languages of the world. And descent by glorifying poverty only digs us further into holes. Ascent and descent is God's business. That is the point of Jesus:

> Though he was in the form of God,
>   he did not deem equality with God something
>   to be grasped at.
> Rather, he emptied himself
>   and took the form of a slave, . . .
> Because of this,
>   God highly exalted him
>   and bestowed on him the name
>   above every other name . . . (Phil 2:6, 7, 9).

The poor, like Tom, are poor in spirit, because poor in fact. They are the anawim, the "emptied" of Yahweh.

The anawim of God were, at first, the Old Testament's migrant workers. They were mobile because the first Israelites were nomads. But these early days of God's people found little distinction between wealth and indigence. In the nomadic Jewish tribes, everyone was equally poor. Family and clan interdependence and some community ownership of lock and stock shielded each one against destitution. But after a while, settlement, individual ownership and expanding econ-

The Poor In Spirit

omy brought wealth; it also brought the depression of peasant and artisan. At this stage, the law gave some protection for the poor; but the poor, Yahweh's anawim, were often pushed aside and down. They became outsiders to the nation's goods and thereby torn from the cloth of God's people as remnants.

It was then that the prophets howled. Amos screamed of the merchants' barter:

> Thus says the Lord:
> . . . I will revoke my word;
> Because they sell the just man for silver
>   and the poor man for a pair of sandals.
> They trample the heads of the weak
>   into the dust of the earth
>   and force the lowly ones out of the way (Am 2:6-7).

Later, the landed classes were stunned at Ezekiel's words:

> The people of the land practice extortion and commit robbery; they afflict the poor and the needy, and oppress the resident alien without justice (Ez 22:29).

And Jeremiah pitted the justice of Israel's ancestors against the contemporary glut:

> Woe to him who builds his house on wrong,
>   his terraces on injustice;
> Who works his neighbor without pay,
>   and gives him no wages.

21

Brian Miclot

Who says, "I will build myself a spacious house,
    with airy rooms,"
Who cuts out windows for it,
    panels it with cedar,
    and paints it with vermillion.
Must you prove your rank among kings
    by competing with them in cedar?
Did not your father eat and drink?
    He did what was right and just,
    and it went well with him.
Because he dispensed justice to the weak and the poor,
    it went well with him.
Is this not true knowledge of me?
    says the Lord.
But your eyes and heart are set on nothing
    except on your own gain.
On shedding innocent blood,
    on practicing oppression and extortion
                                        (Jer 22:13-17).

The anawim of God were the poor pushed to the fringes of Israel. It was into these fringes that Jesus was born. He grew up with an eye on the anawim and walked in their midst. It was these whom Jesus beatified.

For the poor in spirit whom Jesus blessed were the direct descendents of the anawim of Yahweh. And the poor like Tom, generations away, are poor in spirit because poor in fact. Pushed to the fringes, they are the anawim, the "emptied" of Yahweh. One like Tom is

The Poor In Spirit

not just poor in spirit in the easy sense, the sense we'd most like to believe Jesus meant—those who have money, success or a future, but could live as if they hadn't; or those not possessed by their possessions. After all, we can renounce as well as they. Even the best of Wall Street know the risk of renouncing and not looking back.

Neither does Tom have an issue to drive or cause to champion. Assertiveness workshops would not work because such bandwagons come and go, that is the nature of the band's music and the wagon's wheels. As the former head of the American Psychiatric Association once said, "Many counsellors are recommending a kind of self-gratification [another partner, buying something when depressed, moving] which may work for short-term depression, but does not work for long-term living." In a word, we often expect things and causes to do what things and causes cannot do.

But for the poor, the security of "having" anything is gone. The collateral of a successful past, present or future was dispersed long ago. Not being renouncers, only the poor can figure the mystery of non-violence. They can no longer grasp the sword, but they resort only to the making of peace. The poor in spirit are those through whom only, *only* the power of God can be seen, for the world's powers have emptied them. All that's left is mercy and compassion. All that's left is the kingdom. Thus, they know mercy and compassion as no others can. Their only cause is the kingdom.

Tony

"He always brought us roses," Alice said about Tony that Christmas eve. Alice had come to the tap with forty-two presents. All her friends would sooner or later show up, so she brought all her gifts along. We'd talked about gifts, and good cheer; about the past year, and about Tony's death the month before. "A stubborn Hungarian," was her description of a fisty fellow with heavy black eyebrows and deep-set eyes. He was a veteran for the Yanks in WW II, who had come to America to both flee and fight the Axis, and to find hope. He lived in a dingy upstairs apartment a block from the tavern.

Stubborn, talking little except to Vic the bartender, Tony resisted hand-outs and insisted on working. Vic and he had even reached an agreement: he'd clean the alley behind the bar for $5 a day or for a twelve-pack. He'd always worked or paid or fought his way with stubborn pride. Now, pride had left him with a single-roomed stench, an ache for the bottle, and, at last, with death. I told Alice about last autumn, when Tony had looked at me with his deep, blood-bathed eyes and said he'd had the jitters. "The time is near," he said, "I can tell." Two weeks later, death fought him his final bout and won.

The Poor In Spirit

I didn't know about Tony's roses until that Christmas eve with Alice. I went to search for his rosebed later the following spring and found it. The flowers sprayed from the foundation cracks of an abandoned, but elegant Victorian house in the city. The house set on the alley where Tony walked and worked, several blocks from the tavern. The scattered seed of wealthy gardens became Tony's last delight: roses for his ladies.

Somehow, I believe the flowers were signs of hope for Tony and for the other poor of his world. They somehow saw what others couldn't. Through the cemented infra-structures of society, life's gifts bloom. Tony saw. He could gather, and then he could give. And on a cold Christmas eve, Alice remembered what few others could see beneath Tony's heavy, hardened veneer which life seemed to have beaten thick: kindness, brightness and hope. "He always brought us roses."

* * * * * *

Tony and Alice and Tom—the poor in spirit—teach us something, I believe. They teach us, first of all, that the beatitudes are not so much our doing, as God's. It is not so much our working harder to become poor in spirit, or merciful. One does not "try harder" to be truly sorrowful and mourn. And self-esteem seminars do not *give* us the courage to be meek. It is rather that God teaches us through grief and courage and the poor to seek the Lord first, and to rely on the Lord at all times. Letting go and letting God is not the opposite of action or accountability for one's life. Nor is it synonymous with escape. What the poor, the meek and the true grievers teach us is what our faith has always proclaimed: God is in charge. When all is said and done, when our socks are down at night (in all our naked honesty), even in the moment of our greatest accomplishment, the faith of the "blessed" ones speaks the greatest truth: the Lord is Lord alone.

The most "take-charge" person I know is a nurse who directs pediatric units in a large hospital. She seldom displays her "weak moments" and "weak sides" but knows them dearly. With crippling ailments herself and "high stress" days, she walks on faith and is sustained by the prayer her deceased father once taught her: "Work as if everything depended on you; pray as if everything depended on God."

The real task of the beatitudes, then, the real work to be done in practicing the way of Christ is, first of all, God's work. Roses growing through cement or kindness through Tony's tough hide, can only speak of God's command and power:

"I planted the seed and Apollos watered it, but God made it grow. This means that neither he who plants nor he who waters is of any special account, only God, who gives the growth (I Cor 3:6-7).

26

The Poor In Spirit

The kingdom belongs to those who first of all realize their need for God. For the Lord is Lord alone.

Secondly, the poor in spirit, and the other beatitudes teach us in faith that we do not always know what only God can show. The anawim of Yahweh have learned that they can know nothing for certain; they know nothing of tomorrow except that God has something in store. Security for them is only the love of God which beats the sunrise to its shining. We do not always know; only God can show.

Those who do not wait for God's showing or will not patiently seek the epiphany of the Lord—are deceived. Knowledge and decisions which do not wait on the Lord, do not find blessing. We are not even to judge who are blessed and who are not. Think about it. Timidity and lack of courage often disguise as meekness. The cruelest terrorist can believe she is making peace, eventually. And those who cannot let go their grief, i.e., those who cannot mourn, can never know comfort. Remember Donna. She might have been conning Tom with her tears for free rent. And the constant conning among the deprived demands a hermeneutic of the street. But Tom did not judge. He always waited for judging; he deferred. What he did, though, was comfort and house and give rest. We do not always know; only God can show.

Lastly, the greatest lesson of the poor in spirit is found in the testamony of Jesus' own life. It was not only that he himself was poor with ''no place to lay his head'' (Lk 8:20), it was also and most importantly that the ''empty space'' of his poverty was a place *for all*. His *kenosis*, his self-emptying sung about in the early Christian communities, became, in human terms, the opening out of his arms to embrace and save all people for the Father. Notice, for example, that more than a dozen times the scripture tells of Jesus' cohorting with ''those *outside* the law.'' In these passages, he was not condoning the tax-extortion of Matthew; he was calling forth a new man. The scripture says nothing of an affair with Magdalene; it proclaims the humanity loved by God which the pharisees couldn't see. And the reason they couldn't see was that they excluded, they closed off, they remained *filled* with the deadwood planks of their own selves, and so they remained blind. *In*-cluding only their own, they *ex*-cluded mercy. Thus, mercy was not theirs.

On the other hand, Jesus' poverty led him to touch and heal and raise up: ''. . . power went out from him.'' But first, it seems, he was friend and companion (meaning ''with-bread''). He was one who walked alongside the poor and one with whom they broke bread. Their bread was his bread and then the contrary. Jesus' self-emptying poverty was the practice of a woman tenderly gathering the children of God. It was the shepherding-look for the lost. It was a growing in

The Poor In Spirit

the kind of wisdom before God and humanity which learned to see all humanity as though they were his kin, his body, his own flesh and blood. It was a developmental non-exclusion. The lesson of the poor in spirit, the lesson of Jesus' comradery with "tax-collectors and sinners and those outside the law," the lesson of Tom and Alice and Tony is non-possessive, non-exclusive compassion: a "being-and-feeling-with" that excludes no one.

The poor possess only the kingdom. On the contrary, those who clutch or hold on dearly to anything can never receive. When someone holds something in their hands, when their hands are full, there is no place in their hands to put anything. Remember the experiment in which monkeys were given food from a hole only big enough to extend their empty hands through. If they would let go of the food given them on the other side, an experimenter would give them food inside their cage. The results were revealing. Once they grasped food through the hole, they wouldn't let go. Their hands, filled with food, weren't able to come back through the hole. And although the food was subsequently offered to them from within, they wouldn't release what they had clutched. If the experiment continued, they died.

It is much like that with the kingdom. Clutching-on never leads to nourishment. But the poor in spirit possess only the kingdom. They can give only what God has put into their hands or placed beneath their feet or showered into their open arms. Tony gave flowers, Alice gave simple gifts, and Tom his own bed. The kingdom is the mystery, the paradox, which only people like Tom, or Alice, or Tony can call theirs.

The Meek

Bonita Raine

THE cortege wound its way around the corner, turning onto the boulevard, stopping traffic in front of the university whose academic prowess had for over a century assisted a once powerless religious minority to take its place in the boardrooms of corporate America.

The irony was not lost to me as we followed the hearse. Nor was it lost to James Paul's family. "Look at all those people who have come to honor Jimmy!" his sister said. "It looks like so many when they all get into cars. And all the other traffic is stopping for us."

"Yes," I said to his sister, who, with the rest of his family for some years had been separated from J.P.—I called him J.P."; somehow the juxtaposition with the powerful likes of J.P. Morgan was an amusement to both of us when he was alive. The family separation was a nearly tragic circumstance for all of them, born of the misunderstanding and prerogatives unfairly exercised by care-givers over persons whom the system

calls severely retarded. But in the end we were all together—J.P. and I, his family, those who had come to
know him and these strangers who watched us pass
by wondering, no doubt, who was important enough
to be buried during this evening rush hour.

"It seemed almost fitting that those who refused to
notice him in life must stop and take notice in death,"
I thought as the funeral procession of J.P.'s many
friends moved slowly, almost reverently from the small
charismatic church which celebrated his memory one
final time to the historic cemetery overlooking the river.
It reminded me of something I'd read in Simon Tugwell's exposition of the beatitude, "Blessed are the
meek for they shall inherit the earth."

> If it is the meek, the helpless, the disabled, who will in-
> herit the earth, this is perhaps because the earth, the real
> earth, can be had on no other terms. It is a gift. Or, in
> the words of the beatitude, it is an inheritance. And the
> only achievement required for an inheritance is the
> achievement of a death...But life is a gift, a gift always—
> as a gift must be—given without thought of arithmetic
> (Romans 6:23), (1980:37).

At that moment I knew precisely what Tugwell was
challenging us to see: the essential message of the
gospel, which is nothing less than free gift. It exacts
from us a conviction to live as gifted, to force no one's
hand, to answer the call of Jesus, who suggests that

we trust him enough to know that the gift is realized most completely and exhaustively as inheritance.

I knew then at one level that J.P. had received his inheritance. But the inheritance he received was not because of a romantic notion of how persons with severe disabilities in one way or another stumble unwittingly into the kingdom by some inherent innocence. Rather, J.P.'s inheritance came as gift, a blessing which fixed forever in my mind the understanding of Jesus' benediction of the meek, the gentle—promising that they would inherit the earth. The beatitude which gave me comfort then can be understood well by those who know that the inheritance of the earth only comes to those who forswear taking it by force even in the face of their position of privilege as "the afflicted."

To understand that particular position about the beatitude, it is useful to unravel its roots in the poetry of the Hebrew scriptures and its relationship to the tradition to the people of Israel. We must locate it also in the context of Jesus' proclamation of the kingdom and the "upside down" values which were part and parcel, not only of his preaching, but of the meaning of his life and death. There are at least three things we must do if we are to grasp these values and come to a deeper understanding of the beatitude. First, we must see that it is God's sovereign choice which establishes value; often what God values is not what the world values. Secondly, we need to understand that what the world calls "weakness" can, in fact, be a legitimate and tangible representation of the character of God. Finally, we must be convinced that weakness is a prerequisite for the imitation of the God-life and the reception of an inheritance which is, at its heart, gift, neither deserved nor merited.

There is one final notion which suggests itself to us and that is the role which affliction plays in generating the meekness and gentleness of which the beatitude speaks. It is only when we are in touch with our affliction—or that of others—that we become tame enough, gentle enough to know our need to receive an inheritance. And the beatitude is about inheritance, though not exclusively about afterlife. While it does indeed have an eschatalogical tone, Jesus proclaimed the "nowness" of a kingdom—that which was within: the very life of God.

The "Afflicted One" in the Poetry
and Tradition of Israel

It is not revelatory to suggest that when Jesus proclaims, "Blessed are the meek for they shall inherit the earth" he is quoting the thirty-seventh psalm. What may not always get discussed, however, is the identity of the "meek" in the life of Israel and the relevance of that for contemporary reflection.

An analysis of psalm 37 gives us an indication of the

psalmist's conviction. In the face of seeming injustice, the prosperity of the wicked, the psalmist claims that there will be ultimate vindication for the dispossessed. The *anawim* will inherit the land. Tugwell defines these *anawim* as "the underdogs, the people who lack social, political, economic power, the people who are not in a position to control their own circumstances, who cannot pull strings. The people who, on the face of it, stand no chance whatsoever of inheriting the earth" (1980:31). While *anawim* is often translated as "the poor," it is variously translated as "afflicted," "meek," "gentle." It is interesting that we see a curious evolution from a mere situation ("affliction") to a moral notion ("gentleness"). Studying the psalm gives us the opportunity to trace the former sense; thinking of J.P. gives us the opportunity to do that in the latter sense.

When the psalmist writes that "the *anawim* will inherit the land" (37:11), he is claiming that those who are the "afflicted" and the "oppressed," those who prefer to *suffer* wrong than to *do* wrong, will have their inheritance in long cherished promises. The text of the psalm itself assists us in seeing the move from the literal state (i.e., affliction) to a moral category of attitude and behavior (i.e., meekness, gentleness). The ninth verse states that "those who *hope* in Yahweh shall inherit the land." Thus the psalmist exhorts the community of the afflicted to understand that it is not the injustice they suffer which gives them any compensatory right

35

to the land even in the face of violence done to them, but rather their ability to trust in the promise which is bestowed, not appropriated.

It is useful to consider the significance of the image of "the land" and its meaning as inheritance. In the ancient world, one of the few things worth passing along to the next generation was property; it is no accident, after all, that we call it *"real* estate." For the people of Israel, the land was *the* primary promise of Yahweh. "Come to the land I will show you," Yahweh beckoned Abraham; it was the land that became the reward for the steadfast love of faithfulness to the Sinai covenant; it was return to the land that filled the hearts of exiled Jews as they longed from Babylon to be established anew in the place of their inheritance. There were few images as potent as "the land" to symbolize for Israel what it meant to be a people who were to receive an inheritance.

And so we see that if the inheritance of the land functioned to persuade Israel of its ultimate meaning as a people, to be patient must have been no small task, especially when others had taken it from their hands. To trust another for one's vindication is challenging enough when confronted with the bold, mocking oppression of one's enemy, but to forswear pressing one's claims when it might be quite opportune to do so is a constraint of another dimension. The virtue of which the psalmist speaks is an attitude of the heart which trusts sufficiently to place not only one's fate for the present in another's hands, but one's future estate and existence in the hands of another as well. And what the psalmist tries to teach us is, if one is gentle and tender and loving in the midst of it all, the future and one's stake in it, no matter how remote, is assured.

For those faithful in Israel, God's voice and activity to vindicate was as sure and complete as the psalmist could have hoped. Abraham Heschel gives one example when he speaks of the mission of the prophets. "Prophecy," he writes, "is the voice that God has lent to silent agony, a voice of the plundered poor" (1962:5). While God enjoins silence on the oppressed, his call on the lives of others is of another sort. In loving response to the enduring obedience of *anawim* he raises up those who are to identify with and speak for the other. The prophetic voice is raised for the afflicted, not because they are incapable of raising their own voice, but because God has placed a higher call on their lives: the call of faith, the call to trust in his higher purpose, the call to see the glorious work that is his so as to receive "gift" from him and proclaim that he has been the redeemer of his people.

His purpose is realized, as well, as he has recruited others to serve those in need, to identify with the afflicted and to raise the cry of judgment against the injustice done by those who seek to usurp the inheritance of God's chosen ones. And this prophetic voice, even as it raises the righteous judgment of God against those who afflict, can only be done with a heart that is gentle and meek as the psalmist enjoins. The true prophet recognizes that he is merely an instrument, speaking not a word of his own, but only as God speaks, careful to be discerning and accurate, humbled before the awesome responsibility to be a vessel, in whose words, as Abraham Heschel says, again, "God is raging."

In Robert Bolt's recent screenplay, "The Mission," two of his characters live out with ambiguity the struggle to be the voice of God's righteousness on behalf of the afflicted. The two Jesuits' ministry to the Guarani Indians, and the very life they had all built together was threatened by the impending encroachment of colonial oppressors. Facing almost certain destruction of the mission, the Guarani and themselves, they wage deep and personal battles of conscience. Are they called or even permitted to take arms to defend the afflicted ones to whom they minister? Bolt's portrayal of their exchange captures with poignancy the dilemmas to which the psalmist invites us: " 'Remember this, Mendoza,' Father Gabriel said hoarsely, 'If you die with blood on your hands you will die a traitor. You swore to give your life to God, and God is love. . . . If might is right, love has nothing to do in the world. And it may be so,' he reflected heavily. 'It may be so. But I haven't the fortitude to live in a world like that, Mendoza' " (1986:249,261-2).

The Meek

Father Gabriel knew that God's purposes for the Guarani were greater than the existence of the mission he had given them. He knew that those purposes could only be achieved with means which were consistent with those ends. To take up arms to assure that end was self-defeating in his view. Called to forswear being the vindicator, his death was not an act of pietistic quietism, but obedient gentleness, the guarantor of his inheritance.

It does not stretch the point to suggest a common theme in the lives of Father Gabriel, Mendoza, the Guarani or even J.P. The death of each was not their entree to inheritance in the biblical sense, though it was the occasion surely enough. Rather, inheritance, as the psalmist speaks of it, has a moral character; it finds its way into life lived in a particular manner. While it is not incumbent on the lives of the afflicted to accept their lot, for in fact by definition it is not irreversible, the moral demand is to be gentle and trusting while expectantly waiting to see the activity of God on their behalf. Like the two Jesuits, the Guarani of the story, or J.P., there are many who have no chance of inheriting the earth. There are nonetheless those among the dispossessed who have pretensions to power. There are many who join themselves together in the face of racial, economic, political or social injustice for the purpose of asserting their right, of pressing their claim to inheritance. Embittered by the success and esteem which the world affords to their oppressors, they seek the vindication which ought to be theirs.

It is, however, the teaching of the psalm and the beatitude that the contrary is the strategy of God's people. He alone is their vindicator and the inheritance is not theirs to stake a claim on. It is in fact a free gift. "Time rather than power, is on the side of the righteous," Tugwell notes (1980:32).

It is precisely that which J.P. taught me when he was alive. While many might argue that a person with severe handicaps has no choice but to accept his/her lot in life, J.P.'s example led me to understand that such was not the case. Even though he was cognitively quite alert, he had few words and was not independently mobile. I came to understand fairly rapidly how he could have done much more to press his claims against those who represented oppressive systems and personalities to him, if he had chosen. He simply refused to be embittered, though I knew much in his life saddened him. He refused to be non-compliant, though I knew for him the temptation was great. On a regular basis I could see him struggle with wanting to give up rather than affording God, and all of us who cared for him, more time in order to make things better. Yet with a meek and gentle spirit he gave us all time. Time, of course, is a precious commodity to an American of the eighties and yet for the afflicted to offer time is, in fact, to exchange suffering for the meagerness and ineffectual nature of our efforts on their behalf. It is not a neutral gift, but rather one whose moral character is charged with virtue and whose unconditional nature cries out for admiration.

Acknowledging the Sovereign Nature of God's Choice

While it is certainly not the case that we ought to esteem affliction or permit continued devaluation of people for the sake of their receiving the promises of God, the Hebrew scriptures and the teaching of Jesus both lead us to the conclusion that God's choice is directed toward them in a particular way. While God has compassion because of the lot of the afflicted—the scripture tells us, "the Lord was moved to pity by their groaning because of those who oppressed and afflicted them" (Jg 2:18b)—his choice of the afflicted is more often because of the attitude of the heart which they demonstrate. Yahweh speaks through Isaiah, "But to this one I will look, to him who is *aniy* (afflicted, gentle, meek) and of a broken spirit, and who trembles at my word" (66:2b). God's words in the prophet's mouth suggest his active, deliberate seeking out of the afflicted whose spiritual condition of being gentle and meek becomes a prerequisite for receiving from God.

Isaiah is replete with numerous examples of God's choice of the afflicted as the recipients of God's favor (11:4; 29:19; 32:7), but probably nowhere is it more graphic than when Jesus quotes the prophet in his inaugural sermon in the Nazareth synagogue proclaiming his purpose "to bring good news to the afflicted ...bind up the brokenhearted, to proclaim liberty to captives, and freedom to prisoners" (61:1; Lk 4:18). It is the inheritance of the afflicted to receive from God.

It is the character of inheritance to be a free gift of one generation to the next. It is surely a mistake for any of us to assume that we have a right or a claim on the inheritance. It is the sort of flawed thinking which characterizes the demands of both sons in Jesus' parable of the prodigal (Lk 15:11-32). While the one son believes he has a right to the estate, the other son feels he has a right to more than the profligate because he has never neglected his father. The truth is, no matter what is given to the sons, it is given because the father chooses to, not because they have any claims on his possessions.

Likewise, God's choice is sovereign. The fact that he has championed the cause of the afflicted when they have been meek and gentle enough to trust in him should not surprise us in the scriptures. What may tend to surprise us, however, is how God's choice gets translated into contemporary experience. Those whom the world values may not necessarily be those God values. While we can speak in the abstract of the "afflicted," the "meek" and the "gentle," can we claim with equal enthusiasm the "homeless," the "severely disabled", the "victim of AIDS"? What the world forsakes, God embraces.

J.P. was a valued and cherished friend, yet with his moderately impaired intellect and his severely deformed body, I heard more than one person question the worth of his continued existence. The shame of it all was that he heard them, too, and painfully understood.

The Activity and Character of God

Perhaps the greatest shame of all was not that J.P. heard questions about his value; don't we all too frequently ask that question of our own worth? Rather, the shame of it was that God heard, for it is a part of God's character to somehow suffer with those who suffer. The anthropomorphic imagery, while it is that, does tell us something of who God is with and for us. "Metaphors matter," says Terence Fretheim (1984:1 ff). They not only inform our sense of who God is, they are a product of it. "In all their affliction," says Isaiah again, "He was afflicted and the angel of his presence saved them; in his love and in his mercy he redeemed them; and he lifted them and carried them all the days of old" (63:9). If we are to believe Isaiah, and I suggest we ought, our God is a suffering God.

In Fretheim's Old Testament exposition of the character of God he continues:

> God sees the suffering from the inside; God does not look
> at it from the outside, as through a window. God is in-
> ternally related to the suffering of the people. God enters
> fully into the hurtful situation and makes it his own. Yet
> while God suffers with the people he is not powerless
> to do anything about it (1984:128).

Believers and non-believers alike are somehow scandalized by the thought that God might suffer. After
all isn't that notion an affront to our affirmation of an
omniscient and omnipotent God? The heart of our difficulty is an inherent problem with admitting any positive role for suffering at all. Can we admit that our
God suffers? Can we admit that our God identifies with
the afflicted? Can we admit that our God is identified
wholly and inextricably with Jesus? Can we admit it
was Jesus' purpose to assume humanity's affliction and
deal with it exhaustively and irrevocably? Can we admit that it was not only the subject of Jesus' preaching
but the substance of his activity to forswear claims of
divine prerogative so that in meekness and gentleness
he could trust the purposes of Yahweh for the sake of
humanity for all time?

Nowhere in the Christian scriptures is God's activity in this regard portrayed more graphically than in
Paul's letter to the Phillippian church. The text begins,
"If there is any encouragement in Christ, if there is
any consolation of love—have this attitude in yourselves which was also in Christ Jesus, who, although

The Meek

he existed in the form of God, did not regard equality with God a thing to be grasped, but emptied himself, taking the form of a bond servant, and being made in the likeness of men. And being found in appearance as a man, he humbled himself by becoming obedient to the point of death, even death on a cross. Therefore also God highly exalted him'' (2:1, 5-9b).

This text is often used to justify quietism in the face of suffering. While that interpretation may be arguable, I would like to suggest something more. The passage extols Jesus' emptying *(kenosis)* of himself. The hymn celebrates the fact that as Jesus, for the sake of human beings, separated himself from the privilege that was his—from those things he could justly claim as his own—so that he could be available to the purposes of God, the Father indeed could restore him to an even more exalted position. I would like to argue that the principle of *kenosis* has applicability both for those of us who are suffering and for those of us who want to be people of compassion in the face of suffering. Doesn't the spiritual principle of *kenosis* suggest that redemption comes when we are finally able to separate ourselves from the privileges which can rightly be said to belong to those who suffer—righteous indignation, a desire for vindication in the face of the oppressor, etc. If one is willing to be emptied of all one's attitudes concerning the one who afflicts or oppresses, one can finally be in a position to receive the inheritance which is promised. Blessed are the "meek," the "gentle," the "empty."

Weakness as Imitation of the God-life

If it is the "meek," the "gentle," the "empty" who inherit the earth, there is a clear implication for the use of power among the afflicted. In fact the scripture suggests that true power can only be manifested in weakness. The text, which argues for the spiritual significance of weakness, is a short one. Paul writes of his pleading with God to remove a tormenting physical impairment. He experiences God's response, " 'My grace is sufficient for you, for power is perfected in weakness.' Most gladly, therefore, [Paul continues] I will rather boast about my weaknesses, that the power of Christ may dwell in me. Therefore I am well content with weakness. . . for Christ's sake, for when I am weak, then I am strong" (II Cor. 12:9-10).

In this second Pauline passage we are taught that the indispensible link between our suffering selves and the power of God is the acknowledgement of our personal weakness. The apostle teaches us from his own experience of the Lord that only when we have come to the end of ourselves is it possible to experience God's good intentions toward us.

Arthur McGill (1968:47-57) argues this precise point when he explains that Jesus, who is the power of God, contradicts all our assumptions about power not only by championing the weak, but by showing himself as utterly weak. Powerlessness in the Christian story is graphically juxtaposed to the pretentious claims of a power which can do nothing but deceive and oppress. Powerlessness in the Christian story relates to the emptying and pouring out of one's life which is service for the afflicted. Powerlessness in the Christian story is the imitation of the God-life which is constant and complete giving of self without regard to one's rights or privileges. Powerlessness in the Christian story is waiting and trusting for complete vindication by the Holy One as Jesus did during his sojourn in the tomb.

The very life and heart of God which is so manifest to us finds its most telling expression in the cross, not in power. "Our temptation is, and always has been," Simon Tugwell writes, "to try to achieve God's purposes by using the methods of the world. But any such attempt is shut off by the cross of Christ" (1980:38). The cross is for Christians not only a revelation of the true heart and strategy of God towards humanity, but it is the way God chose to re-establish, once and for all, the value of that humanity. And so the cross has moral value, because it will be the way, *par excellance,* through which Christians can most effectively relate to the afflicted. It is not merely a consoling representation of the burdens they bear in this life that are likened to, or given meaning by, the sufferings of Jesus.

Rather the cross is a way of knowing God and being one with the will of the Father. To pour out one's life for an afflicted one, particularly in the face of the opposition of the oppressor, is in fact to establish the value of the one who is cared for. The giving of life on behalf of another is to lift the existence of the other to a new plane, even if that requires suffering, grief or affliction on the part of the one who gives life. The moral significance of the cross for Christians who spend themselves for others is not only the suffering and loss they bear in the process, but the fact that they embrace a moral ideal which may run counter to the wisdom and the values of the world. When the world outside would ask them why they would do such a thing, they know that the value which God in Jesus establishes to their action is indeed close to the heart of God who spent himself in a similar way historically so many years before. They know, in fact, that not only have they become imitators of the acts of God, but the very nature of God.

Gentleness and Inheritance:
A Contemporary Challenge

I am persuaded that without identification with the afflicted we will never be gentle in the sense of the beatitude, hence, not gifted with inheritance.

Since the moral cost of Christian discipleship derives

from its origin in covenant commitment, Christianity finds fulfillment of that commitment in the notion that Yahweh invested heavily in human life by radically identifying himself with it in Jesus Christ. Thus, not only is there a presumption on behalf of humanity inherent in the Christian story, there is a sense that as one identifies with others even in their affliction, one is doing something God-like and thus intrinsically faithful and moral. In fact it is the role of religious faith to speak to people concerning the commitments which they have for one another both in the community and outside the community. It is those very commitments, offered for certain ultimate reasons, which become the alleviator of affliction, the tender of mercies, the sustainer of lives, even when life appears on the surface to be so broken. It is that very set of commitments which has the potential to make one gentle in the sense of the beatitude.

Like so many things in life generally, commitment offers mutual benefit. It is not only the pouring out of life, but it is the reception of life. It is not only the bearing of burdens, but it is being carried aloft as well. It is not only the nurturing of life and faith, but it is being awakened to new possibilities of trust. Persons who are weak and dependent and afflicted actually become images for us of personal faith, and so we are strengthened. Since faith represents dependence on the plans and promises of another, we see *in* their dependence a paradigm for the trusting relationship which the scripture names "faith." Faith suggests that it is actually all right to believe that spending ourselves now on behalf of those to whom we are committed will have ultimate significance. Hence, we will not only act to relieve the affliction of the oppressed, but because of the resources that he calls forth from us, we will become as they are—the gentle who will inherit the earth.

References

Bolt, Robert. *The Mission* (New York: Berkeley Publishing Group) 1986.

Fretheim, Terence E. *The Suffering of God: An Old Testament Perspective* (Philadelphia: Fortress Press) 1984.

Heschel, Abraham. *The Prophets: An Introduction* (New York: Harper & Row) 1962.

McGill, Arthur C. *Suffering: A Test of Theological Method* (Philadelphia: The Geneva Press) 1968.

Tugwell, Simon. *The Beatitudes: Soundings in Christian Traditions* (Springfield, IL: Templegate Publishers) 1980.

The Sorrowful

Sheila Cassidy

IT SEEMS to me that there have been three distinct stages in my encounter with the beatitudes—three different levels of engagement and understanding. The first level was the easiest, the coziest and the most superficial: it is the level of appreciation of the poetry, the counterpoint and the paradox. At first hearing one thinks, "how lovely," how reassuring, how true; one's heart warms and one feels comforted. And that is good. For the words *are* beautiful and poetic and true, and have a power to lift the heart.

The second encounter came to me many years later, when I had the courage to question words and concepts which I had always accepted simply because they were in the gospel. It came at a time when I was split wide open by the terrible reality of suffering: by the hunger of the Third World, the pain and impotence of the oppressed and the weariness and despair of the incurably sick. These were in truth, the sorrowful: the Ethiopian woman whose shrunken breasts were a dried up water hole for her dying baby; the man held head down in a bath of filth because he would not betray his friends; and the doctor of 22 with the brain tumor, cut off like a wild flower as her face was turned towards the sun.

Who dares call these people blessed, for when and in what green lands will they find consolation? Will the relief workers arrive in time to save the Ethiopian woman? Will her breasts fill again with milk and her baby gurgle with delight? Or will she, like thousands of others, drop silently to the ground, too weak even to weep for the dead child in her arms? Will her bones whiten in the sun alongside those of the cattle, a silent witness to the harshness of nature, the immutability of bureaucracy and monstrous injustice of a divided world?

And what of the freedom fighter, the guerrilla, the revolutionary? Will the excrement in his lungs be replaced by clean air, or will he too die of pneumonia, his ribs kicked in and his hands crushed by interrogators blinded by fear, hatred and indoctrination?

And what of the fat cats, the politicians, the generals, the businessmen in their capital cities, racked by a sorrow so deep they cannot even touch it, cannot name it, a sorrow that can only be expressed as greed and a lust for power. When, and in what time and place will *they* find consolation? Or will they remain forever hungry, manipulators of men, blind to the sun and the stars until they plunge deeper and deeper into the pit of their own avarice and stupidity?

The Sorrowful

And the sick, the handicapped, the broken, so much more accessible to us in the "developed" world: will their cancers vanish, the pain go, their mutilated bodies be restored to wholeness? Will they leap for joy and dance again—or will they fade, their limbs shrunken and their bellies swollen until they are indistinguishable from the Ethiopian, the prisoner and the refugee? When will their mourning be turned into joy, their sorrow into consolation?

Today? Tomorrow? In heaven—or never? Do the beatitudes promise hope of resurrection—or pie in the sky to comfort the bystanders, to release us from the pain of responsibility, of solidarity, of being a member of the human race? I have no answer to these awkward, almost blasphemous questions, save the conviction that they must be asked. If we Christians do not ask them, the unbelievers certainly will, and there can be no meeting point unless we have the courage for dialogue.

My first experience of such questioning began in prison when I was joined in the solitary confinement block of a Santiago prison by a girl of 19 called Lelia. Highly intelligent and a Marxist, with a mind far more open and enquiring than my own, Lelia was determined to put her captivity to good use. Quite unashamedly, she set about me, not to convert, but to learn what I believed. What was this Christianity about? What use was it to turn the other cheek—was this not just capitalistic propaganda to keep the poor in their place, to stop them from rising up to claim their rightful inheritance? I can't remember how I handled her questions—only that I struggled to answer honestly in my broken Spanish and squirmed at the forthrightness of her questioning. I remember too that I loved her, so young, so honest, so serious—and so given to the poor of her land.

My own experience of questioning, however, came much later when I began to work with the dying. For me, reflection and questioning of my faith came very late, and I experienced a certain degree of wheel wobble. A period of stress and depression led me into conversation with a psychologist and as I explored the forces that drive me, I was forced to question my own personal salvation history and the belief that God had called me to his exclusive service from my youth. As I pieced together the fragments of memory of a wartime childhood and an adolescence marked by hero worship of nuns and priests, I realized that my "vocation" had a very human basis to it as well as—if not instead of—a divine. With my foundations thus rocked, I turned slowly to face the whole of my belief system, wondering if it would collapse like some elaborate card house and leave me weeping amidst the ruins.

For a while, I sat in the fog, becalmed, lost, literally not knowing if I believed in God or not. At 47 I was plunged into adolescent questioning, wondering if the cynical jest "and in the beginning, man created God," could possibly be true. There is no dramatic beginning

The Sorrowful

or end to my agnostic period—it came upon me gradually like a patch of mist and lifted just as unexpectedly a few months later. It has left me, as I have heard other people say, believing less but with more conviction, though that conviction itself is a fragile thing and pure gift. With poet Jim Cotter I can say:

I embrace the Law of Loving,
Dying to possessive need
Risen with Christ,
Though crushed by wine press,
Into spacious glory breathed.

"Risen with Christ, though crushed by wine press." What does he mean? Is he speaking simply of the life after death, a life beyond starvation, torture or cancer—or of some liberty of the spirit attainable in this life, inspite of—perhaps even because of—suffering mourning, the crushing between the forces of fate, injustice or disease. I don't know—but I think it has to be both. Just as there is no doubt that some people emerge from suffering to a life of new liberty of spirit, so others are apparently crushed by it, submerged under the weight of bitterness and pain. It seems crucial to me that "believing" people could have the courage to face this aspect of human experience, for to pretend that all are strengthened, purified and liberated by suffering is to be quite out of touch with reality. And a Christianity which is not firmly rooted in reality is not Christianity at all.

When I embarked upon this piece, I had thought to find clear and powerful words about the consolation of the sorrowful. Surely I who have emerged strengthened from the torture chamber and who am in daily contact with the dying must have some answers to the problems of suffering? And yet, when the moment comes, I find myself almost empty-handed. What I offer is a disjointed series of reflections, which may or may not make sense.

The first thing I would say is that I don't really understand what "Blessed" implies. Some translations render it as "happy." Are we to understand this word in its literal sense, or are we talking about some deep spiritual happiness inaccessible at the level of the feelings. God knows, I was not happy in the torture cell nor am I in the midst of the black moods of despair which plague me from time to time. Jean Vanier understands "Blessed" as being somehow specially watched over by God. That I find easier to accept, for I have experienced the presence of God in the midst of atrocious suffering.

During the experience of torture in which intolerable pain was compounded by terror and powerlessness, I was aware of the presence of God in quite a curious way: I felt he was there, alongside, somehow in solidarity with me and yet not taking the pain away. He was just there—not comforting or protecting, but there.

The Sorrowful

In the midst of the squalor of the interrogation center with its harsh guards and filthy lavatories I was no longer an onlooker at the passion but somehow taking part. It was not a great mystical experience—just a rather matter-of-fact appreciation of a reality.

Later on, in solitary confinement, I met God in a quite different way. The torture was apparently over, although I lived in constant terror that the interrogators would begin again. My days were spent in a small room containing two sets of bunks and a chair. I saw the warders briefly when they brought the food or when they let me out to go to the lavatory. Otherwise I was left alone to my thoughts, my fears and whatever prayers I was capable of.

Now, twelve years later, I believe that this three week period of struggle and desolation was of crucial importance, for I see it as a time of naked encounter with God. Like Jacob, I wrestled all night with an unseen stranger and was somehow blessed before he left me, wounded, at daybreak.

> And Jacob was left alone. And there was one who wrestled with him until daybreak who seeing that he could not master him, struck him in the socket of his hip, and Jacob wrestled with him. He said, 'Let me go, for day is breaking.' But Jacob answered, 'I will not let you go unless you bless me.' He then asked, 'What is your name?' 'Jacob' he replied. He said, Your name shall no longer be Jacob, but Israel, because you have been strong against God, you shall prevail against men.' Jacob then

made this request, 'I beg you, tell me your name' but he replied, 'Why do you ask my name?' And he blessed him there.''

Jacob named the place Peniel, 'because I have seen God face to face,' he said 'and I have survived.'

Genesis

Some years ago I came across a quotation from a 19th century philosopher called Stifter. He wrote: ''Pain is a Holy Angel which shows treasure to men which otherwise remains forever hidden.'' I knew at once what he meant and that it was true—although it is one of those mysterious truths which is difficult to explain to others. Dare we say that those who mourn are blessed because they encounter God in a special way— that Stifter's Holy Angel reveals to them a treasure which remains hidden to those whose life takes a smoother, apparently happier course? I believe that this is true—though I am not sure if I can explain why. What did I learn during those three weeks alone?

That night, that year of now done darkness I wretch lay wrestling with (my God!) my God.

G. M. Hopkins
—*Carrion Comfort*

Perhaps I should explain a little about the nature of my struggle, which could, I think, be described in spiritual jargon as an abandonment experience. Although

The Sorrowful

what happened to me occurred in the rather exotic context of a South American gaol, it is, in essence, the same struggle undergone by many people who find themselves trapped by illness or unfortunate personal circumstances. The experience is not about prison per se but about a way of confronting and adapting to a situation from which there is no escape.

After the initial nightmare days of the torture center where I survived from minute to minute, sometimes cowering like a frightened animal and sometimes given powers of endurance that astonished me, I was transferred to another hidden prison called Cuatro Alamos, the solitary confinement block. As the door slammed on me and I found myself alone, I at last had space to think. When the first twenty-four hours elapsed without further interrogation and my most primitive needs of food and sleeping were satisfied, I was able to explore the limits of my inner freedom. Denied more than a few square feet for physical movement, I found that my spiritual space was much larger. It was not long before I found myself reciting Lovelace's poem:

> Stone walls do not a prison make,
> Nor iron bars a cage;
> Minds innocent and quiet take,
> That for an hermitage.
>
> If I have freedom in my love,
> And in my soul am free;

Sheila Cassidy

Angels alone that soar above,
Enjoy such liberty.

To Althea from Prison

In this secret space I found that I had two very clear options. The first was to pray to be let out, and the second was to accept whatever God had in mind for me. In human terms, of course, this was Hobson's Choice—the Lord does whatever he wills, anyway, but in spiritual and psychological terms, the difference it made was enormous.

If we scream to be let out we are like a wild bird in a cage, beating our wings against the bars until we are terrified, bruised and exhausted. All our energy is dissipated in the fight, and we are left spent and useless. If we are able to accept, however, to trust, then not only do we enter into a quite different relationship with God, but we are able to use our psychic energy in a creative rather than in a destructive way.

So this was my battle: between praying to be released and praying for the strength to accept God's Will. It was a drama enacted over the three weeks of my confinement, for although on some days I was able to make an act of acceptance, at other moments I was reduced again to despair and the plea that the cup should be taken from me. My deepest fears were that I should be executed or confined to prison for many years, and I was terrified at either prospect. And yet, eventually, I was able to let go, say my Fiat.

The Sorrowful

Some time during the course of my solitary confinement, I received a visit from the British Counsul who brought me a parcel from my friends. Among the gifts of clothes, soap and chocolate was E.F. Farrell's book, *Disciples and other strangers* which contained in its appendix the following poem:

ABANDONMENT

Father,
I abandon myself into your hands...
What does it mean to abandon oneself to God?

What is an abandonment experience?
Is it leaving oneself on God's doorstep,
  walking into the rest of life,
    not allowing anxiety,
      fear,
      frustration to enter into one?
Is it expecting God to keep one warm,
      secure,
      and safe,
      unharmed?
Is that abandonment?

Abandonment has nothing to do with warmth of
      womb or arms
      or closed clasped hearts.

It is not something done by a child.
It is done to him.
It cannot be done to an adult.
It is done by him.
Abandonment is committed only with and in the
  maturity of Christ Jesus.

Sheila Cassidy

It is not just a hanging loose.
It is a letting go.
It is a severing of the strings by which one
    manipulates,
            controls,
            administrates
        the forces in one's life
Abandonment is managing nothing,
        blocking or blotting out nothing,
            expecting nothing.
Abandonment is receiving all things the way
    one receives
            a gift
        with opened hands,
        and opened heart.

Abandonment to God
    Is the climactic point in any man's life.

There is nothing left to do then.
No place to go.
Death has occurred.
                            Anonymous

What happens during an abandonment experience?
In what sense is it the climactic point in a person's life?
Again, I find it difficult to explain except to say that
one enters into a new relationship with God—that like
Jacob, though wounded, one is somehow blessed. Perhaps the essence is the transference of the knowledge
that God loves us from the level of the intellect to that

The Sorrowful

of the guts. Like Mother Julian, one knows somehow, that, whatever happens, all things shall be well and all manner of things shall be well. One knows that God is there, with one, in fear and danger, in desolation and despair. This is the consolation of those that mourn—they know that God is somehow in their pain and darkness, that they do not walk alone.

It is important to understand that this carnal knowledge of God brings consolation at a level so deep that we can barely touch it, for it is a consolation that can and does co-exist with fear, anxiety, depression and unhappiness. This is one of the great mysteries of the spiritual life: that although closeness to God is a source of unimaginable joy, it does not in any sense protect us from the pain which is an integral part of the human condition. We remain the people we always were, neurotic and fragile, subject to anger, self-pity and dark despair. And yet, there is a difference, which I think is manifested as the virtue of hope. A monk friend of mine makes the distinction between *expectation* and *hope*.

Expectation is that which is likely to happen, given the way things are: A cure is likely, or things can only get worse. Hope, on the other hand, is the knowledge that God can and will bring good out of evil, light out of darkness, life out of death. Hope is the basis of Bonhoeffer's Statement:

Sheila Cassidy

I believe that God can and will bring good out of evil. For that purpose he needs men who makes the best use of everything. I believe God will give us all the power we need to resist in times of distress. But he never gives it in advance, lest we should rely upon ourselves and not upon him alone.

Dietrich Bonhoeffer
Letters and Papers from Prison

I find it fascinating to hear Bonhoeffer, the 20th-century Lutheran pastor imprisoned in Nazi Germany, echoing the words of another German, the 14th-century Dominican mystic, Meister Eckhart. In one of his sermons Eckhart writes boldly of the God who deliberately strips his servants of all their supports and props so that they may rest on him alone.

The faithful God often lets his friends fall sick and lets every prop on which they lean be knocked out from under them. It is a great joy to loving people to be able to do important things such as watching, fasting and the like, besides sundry more difficult undertakings. In such things they find their joy, their stay and their hope. Thus their pious works are supports, stays, footings to them.

Our Lord wants to take all these things away, for he would like to be their only stay. He does this because of his simple goodness and mercy. He wants nothing more than his own goodness. He will not be influenced in the least to give or do by any act of ours. Our lord wants his friends to be rid of such notions. That is why he removes every prop, so that he alone may support them. It is his

The Sorrowful

will to give greatly, but only because of his own free goodness, so that he shall be their support and they, finding themselves to be nothing at all, may know how great the generosity of God is. For the more helpless and destitute the mind that turns to God for support can be, the deeper the person penetrates God and the more sensitive he is to God's most valuable gifts. Man must build on God alone.

Meister Eckhart
Sermon 19

I do not know whether Eckhart is right and whether God deliberately exposes some people to sufferings in order to strengthen them. There is certainly ample precedent for this line of thought in the Old Testament if one considers the story of Job or the Wisdom literature:

My son, if you aspire to serve the Lord,
prepare yourself for an ordeal.
Be sincere of heart, be steadfast,
and do not be alarmed when disaster comes.
Cling to him and do not leave him,
so that you may be honoured at the end of your days.
Whatever happens to you, accept it,
and in the uncertainties of your humble state, be patient,
since gold is tested in the fire,
and chosen men in the furnace of humiliation.

Ecclesiasticus 2:1ff

Sheila Cassidy

If we accept as mystery that perhaps God does test some men in the "furnace of humiliation" we can go on to explore the spiritual and psychological mechanisms by which disaster can be seen, in hindsight, as a gift.

I have scandalized many people by saying that I see my prison experiences as a gift—and perhaps I have unconsciously denied the horror of it in order to escape the pain. Be that as it may, I believe that the experience of being stripped of all one's support systems has two profound effects. The first is that it does in truth force one to rest upon God alone and the second is that it teaches one to understand as gift many things hitherto taken for granted. There is a very real sense in which the poor have the earth for their heritage for when one is stripped of freedom, health, good food, possessions, one rediscovers what a monk friend of mine calls "the essential giveness of things."

Released from pain one becomes grateful not to hurt; hungry, one is grateful for bread and water. I recall hearing a woman who escaped from Auschwitz describe how she ate a tube of toothpaste and found it the most delicious thing she had ever tasted. In prison I found myself praying an extraordinary litany of thanksgiving—for my wholeness of body, for my food, my blanket, for the sparrows with whom I shared my crumbs and for the glimpse of the sunrise gained by standing on a chair at the window of my cell.

The Sorrowful

Of course one does not have to experience prison to learn to value the commonplace. So often one discovers that the most joyous and generous people are those who have experienced severe illness or bereavement. On a recent visit to Corrymeela, a community for reconciliation in Northern Ireland, I met a remarkable woman who, after her son had been shot dead, emerged from her fury and grief to help other bereaved families. She went to the office of the Belfast newspaper, and made a list of the names and addresses of the people who had been killed, and began visiting them.

Almost without exception they greeted her with open arms for they had no one with whom they could talk through their anger and grief. From this beginning there grew a support group which still meets on a regular basis. I marvelled at this woman as she drove me to the airport. Here was someone whose mourning had been not *turned* into joy, but accompanied by it.

This, then is my understanding of the truth that those who mourn shall find consolation. Specially blessed by a God who loves the poor and the powerless, they struggle with him until daybreak. Then, having seen God face to face and survived, they emerge wounded by knowing deep in their guts that he loves them, that all his world is holy ground and that death, when it comes, is quite simply the beginning, not the end.

Those Who Hunger and Thirst for Justice

Rachelle Linner

The strangest thing was the silence. It was one of the most unforgettable impressions I have. You'd think that people would be panic-striken, running, yelling. Not at Hiroshima. They moved in slow motion, like figures in a silent movie, shuffling through the dust and smoke. I heard thousands of people breathing the words, "Water, give me water." Many simply dropped to the ground and died.

Setsuko Thurlow
13-year-old schoolgirl
August, 1945

POLITICAL and military decisions taken by leaders irrevocably change the most basic textures of private lives. One determining historical event in my family was the Russo-Japanese war of 1904. My maternal grandfather left his Russian village so as to avoid conscription in that war. I do not know if he was a pacifist, my philosophical as well as genetic ancestor, but whatever reasons caused him to undertake that arduous journey to an unknown land, I relish the irony that I am an American because of one of Japan's wars. It is another of Japan's wars, the one that ended four decades after the victory over Russia at Port Arthur, the one that ended with the atomic bombings of Hiroshima and Nagasaki, that has become a compelling event for my study, thought and prayer. The weapons that ended that war ushered in the nuclear age I have lived in. More precisely, it is as an American that I approach the suffering that began when those weapons exploded.

Eighty years after my grandfather immigrated to the United States I journeyed to Hiroshima. My task was to interview hibakusha, the survivors of the bomb (the word hibakusha translates literally as explosion-affected person(s)). I sensed that in listening to their stories I would wrestle with what it meant to live in a time of idolatry, enslaved by the bonds of despair that well up when acknowledging what it has meant to develop, use, and continue to stockpile weapons that can destroy all life on earth.

I went to Hiroshima after reading books and articles about World War II. I knew that the bombs were not necessary to end the war and prevent an invasion of the Japanese main islands—the justification offered at the time. Physically and psychologically exhausted by the war, their major cities and industrial capability in ruins from saturation bombings, the Japanese had already made overtures (through the Soviet Union) to

Those Who Hunger and Thirst for Justice

discuss the terms of surrender. I learned that the bombs were used, not against the Japanese, but as a political statement to the Soviet Union (which had entered the Pacific conflict on August 8, 1945) as insurance that the United States would be the sole occupying power of Japan.

With little scientific background I had difficulty understanding the theoretical and many of the practical developments that resulted in these new weapons. Perhaps because of that I concentrated on the drama of this community of scientists, theorists suddenly thrust into proximity of military and political leaders, and of the acts of courage and moral honesty as they wrestled with what they had created. For many, especially those whose lives were changed because of Nazism, the motivation to develop the atom bomb was fear that the Nazis would develop it first—a fear based on the state of pre-war German physics. This was to be proved unwarranted, and Germany was defeated before the bomb was operable. Sixty-three prominent scientists petitioned Truman, urging that he not approve military use of the bomb, arguments they based not only on humanitarian grounds, but on their fears for a future chained to these weapons, the future we inhabit now. I read of scientists who saw themselves "no more guilty than any technician" and those who felt they had known sin.

Most importantly I read hibakusha testimony, trying to absorb these words that simply and directly speak of the terrible destruction they witnessed with a meditative quiet. Facts and figures, reports of the physical and medical costs of the bombs, can overwhelm the student. In the face of chilling litanies of destruction I needed to focus on the human element, to cling to images of human caring, the small moments of those days that changed history.

It was hibakusha testimony that first awakened my heart to Hiroshima's story. I met them for the first time in 1973, when a number of hibakusha were here as part of a larger group of Japanese anti-nuclear activists who presented a petition at the United Nations calling for an end to nuclear weapons. Fifteen years later I remember the inner silence their stories evoked in me—not just their words, but the fact that they were in the United States, gracious to citizens of the nation that had birthed such terrible pain in their lives. I did not know, of course, about the years when they knew a terrible anger and bitterness, the times of despair, the rage that they had been used as guinea pigs, the memories that echoed in their hearts each time another nuclear device was tested.

I did not need to know history or science to know that I was in the presence of people who embodied a new ethic, a new spirit. I learned that their often-repeated statement, "it is war we hate, not Americans," is the "spirit of Hiroshima." It is that vow inscribed on the Memorial Cenotaph in Hiroshima's

Those Who Hunger and Thirst for Justice

Peace Memorial Park: ''Rest in peace; the mistake will not be repeated.'' The living of this vow honors the memory of the hundreds of thousands who died on that day of the unforgettable fire, and of the thousands who have died since, for this is a weapon which kills through time, as the diseases of radiation have continued to claim hibakusha. While they live their survival is imbued with meaning as they witness to what they know. They speak, not to elicit sympathy or to create guilt in their listener, but to warn, a prayer for us, that they alone will know atomic death. Their words are given us at a high price; they not only relate but relive memories.

> My clothes were tattered and covered with blood. I had cuts and scratches all over me, but all of my extremities were there. I looked around me. Even though it was morning, the sky was dark, as dark as twilight. Then I saw streams of human beings shuffling away from the centre of the city. Parts of their bodies were missing. Their eyes had been liquified. They had blackened skin, and strips of flesh hung like ribbons from their bones. There was an awful stench in the air; the stench of burnt human flesh. I can't describe that smell, but it was a bit like broiled fish.
>
> Setusko Thurlow

It is war they hate, not Americans—but for hibakusha, the war has never ended. The signing of the surrender aboard the battleship *Missouri*, the Allied Occupation,

73

the San Francisco Peace Treaty—these are events of history. What hibakusha endure is not only the ill-nesses radiation has caused, but the pain of being ignored in a world that amasses more instruments of death year after year, a world that has been deaf to their pleas, a world that is too proud, too intoxicated with power, to hear their cries for peace. They call us to a radical transformation of heart, because even if we abolish nuclear weapons we will forever know how to build them.

Hiroshima is a place of transformation, a proud military city totally destroyed, a city that "like a phoenix, rose from the ashes" into a mecca of peace that annually draws thousands, who come with their guilt, sorrow, fear and hope to stand, at least symbolically, with hibakusha—the first victims of the nuclear age who are now its prophets.

Thousands died begging for water, gripped by an intense thirst that was never quenched; many died hungry, the sparse stores of a nation exhausted by war diminished still further by the fires that ravaged the bombed cities. The beatitude tells us, "Blessed are those who hunger and thirst for holiness, they shall have their fill." The physical hunger and thirst of those who died has been transformed into a deep, moral, spiritual quest. In their refusal to seek revenge, in the moral power of their witness, hibakusha embody the holiness of radical forgiveness. Their desire for peace

Those Who Hunger and Thirst for Justice

stands in opposition to the suicidal weapons that ring the planet. One hibakusha, Dr. Ichiro Moritaki, articulates this in his phrase ''the chain reaction of spiritual atoms will overcome the chain reaction of material weapons.''

Amid the multiplicity of the world's religions, the one teaching all hold in common is a universality, the world as one community, one people. Ironically, it is radiation that has taught the world this in the most uncompromising terms. Radiation, which respects no national boundaries, kills without regard to race, creed, political persuasion, and certainly without regard to ''combatant'' or ''non-combatant'' status. Radiation from Chernobyl contaminated Lapp reindeer herds 2000 kilometers away, and created ecological, cultural and economic dislocations among the herders in Samiland. Radiation causes cancer in the children of atomic veterans and contaminates crops in land downwind from processing plants.

Radiation has caused the great suffering hibakusha have known, its toll more terrible than even the shock waves that made it seem the earth had split asunder, more than the heat, which for a few seconds reached 7000 degrees Farenheit.

Between August and December, 1945, many people sickened and died from acute radiation sickness. We have contemporary images of this in photographs of Chernobyl victims. Hair falls out, there is bleeding from the mouth and bloody urine and stool; the victims lose all appetite, and suffer from severe vomiting. When tested they are found to be anemic, and to have abnormally low white blood cell counts. During this same time keloid scars developed after treatment of radiation burns, scars that were so thick that they caused underlying muscles to contract, immobilizing arms and legs. Anemia, blood disorders, sterility and abnormal menstruation were common in the first year after the war. Perhaps the most tragic victims were those born in the early months of 1946, the profound physical and mental retardation of the youngest hibakusha, those who had been exposed in their mother's wombs. Leukemia began its scourge through the hibakusha population in 1946; it would peak between 1950 and 1953. Radiation-induced cataracts were first discovered in 1948. In time, malignancies of the thyroid, breast, lung and salivary gland were acknowledged as radiation-related diseases.

The medical effects on the children of hibakusha (second generation hibakusha) are still being studied.

The social and emotional suffering of hibakusha must be added to the result of these two bombs. Thousands of children became "A-bomb orphans," some of whom were taken in by relatives, some cared for in orphanages, but many of whom had to fend for themselves in the profound poverty and social dislocation of the post-war years. (In the months preceding the atomic bombings, many children had been evacuated to the country as a protection against the anticipated "conventional" bombings which Hiroshima had been spared. In many cases, their parents, who had remained in the city, were killed in the bombing.) The social dislocation they endured is mirrored now in the lives of the "orphaned elderly," those whose children and spouses died, and who now have no family to care for them in their aging years.

(The first hibakusha medical relief law was passed in 1957, a complicated system of benefits administered by the central government as a "special social security measure." For many years the city governments of Hiroshima and Nagasaki, and many hibakusha groups, have called for the "completion of A-bomb relief measures" under the national indemnity clause, a critical distinction. The present measures are "charity" but changing the source of funding would recognize that hibakusha have suffered because of a war their government began in 1941. Under terms of the 1952 peace treaty, the United States is exempt from financial liability. In addition to the benefits, which have increased over the years, Japanese hibakusha have access to the highest quality free medical care in hospitals and clinics in Hiroshima and Nagasaki. Unfortunately, similar care is denied American hibakusha (unless they pay for their trip to Japan). Most of them are American citizens of Japanese ancestry who were re-

siding in Japan when the war began. Unable to return
to the United States, the were exposed to the atomic
bombs and eventually repatriated. Efforts to pass leg-
islation calling for medical coverage for American
hibakusha have failed; the defense community is one
of the reasons why. As one American hibakusha re-
marked, "They don't like us because we remind people of what can happen.")

Hibakusha have also had to endure discrimination.
They have been deemed unsuitable marriage partners
for fear that radiation would harm familial blood lines.
Many hibakusha have been denied access to Japan's
economic miracle due to being considered "poor"
workers because of fatigue and their vulnerable health
status. Some hibakusha have not identified themselves
as such to avoid discrimination. Many have chosen to
remain silent. Yet as they age, many hibakusha feel
the need to convey the experience of the atomic bombings. Words can only hint at the enormity of suffering
they witnessed and remember, and this pain, the despair and loneliness, the grief and despair, are spoken
of simply as "keloid of the heart" and "leukemia of
the spirit."

In the Magnificat, Mary proclaims that God has "confused the proud in their inmost thoughts." This is the
attitude that accompanies a society gripped by idolatry,
as ours is by the delusion that nuclear weapons will

Those Who Hunger and Thirst for Justice

bring us "security." The "proud" who perpetuate and profit from these suicidal weapons are not alone in their confusion. There is a double life that people are forced to live. Setsuko Thurlow explained it simply: "We make plans for the future assuming that there will be a tomorrow; at the same time, we know that we and everyone dear to us could be incinerated today." Corporate, no less than personal decisions, are affected—from the re-institution of the death penalty to rapacious environmental decisions, these acts express communal despair and hint at how final the nuclear cataclysm will be.

Individuals are injured by what psychiatrists identify as "psychic numbing," the denial of what it means to live in the nuclear age, a spiritual malaise of despair that results from the possibility that the world, in all its achingly beautiful and transient loveliness, could disappear. People are afflicted with a helplessness, similar to that of a person who dies because a spell is cast upon them. The lack of hope, the sense of "what is the use" allows the nuclear culture to invade our "inmost thoughts" and the grip of despair tightens.

Hibakusha have mobilized the complex emotions engendered by their experience of the bombs to witness, by example, by word and deed, that it is possible to overcome the helplessness and powerlessness that feed the nuclear demon. One of the most powerful moments I experienced in Hiroshima was the story of a hibakusha, told to me by his daughter. We were walking in his garden as she spoke, a plethora of flowers and bonsai trees nurtured on the steep slopes behind their home. She told his story, one he has shared only within the confines of his family, and spoke of her own yearning for peace as a child of hibakusha. Her father had tended his garden through thirty years of Sunday afternoons, a garden he planted a decade after he had cremated, in another garden, his atom-bomb killed mother. He has lived an anonymous, happy life, with a good marriage, healthy children, and is a respected member of his office staff. The existence of this garden, its verdant beauty, its richness and abundance, became the vehicle through which I received the inestimable gift of hope. Moved as I was by the starkly eloquent monuments in the Peace Park and the courage evinced by hibakusha testimonies, this hidden garden came to symbolize the regeneration of a city that likens itself to a ''phoenix rising from the ashes.''

When hibakusha speak they reclaim the human dimension from the anonymity imposed by technological warfare. Amidst statistics of incomprehensible destruction individual suffering affects the listener most acutely, because it is the human dimension that restores the kinship that war, racism and nationalism destroy.

Those Who Hunger and Thirst for Justice

At the foot of the hill was an army training ground. Every inch of it was covered with the dead and dying. There were tens of thousands of them, groaning and begging for water. Those of us who could walk went down and tried to help. They were suffering the most terrible sensation of heat and dehydration. Everybody wanted water. We didn't, however, have cups or containers to carry water. We went to the nearby stream and took off our blouses and soaked them. Then we rushed back and put the cloths over the mouths of the dying. They desperately sucked at the moisture. That was all we could do.

Setsuko Thurlow

Dr. Tadatoshi Akiba, a professor at Hiroshima Shudo University, has had a deep interest in conveying the human cost of the atomic bomb. He attributes his life-long interest in issues of war and peace to childhood memories (at age two-and-a-half) when he was exposed to air raids over his home in Chiba, a city not far from Tokyo, memories that were reawakened when, as an elementary school student, he saw the film "Children of the Atomic Bomb." His education gave him an image of the United States as a country of "democracy and idealism" an image somewhat shaken while an American Field Service student, and the mere mention of Hiroshima would bring an almost automatic response: Pearl Harbor.

Like many of his contemporaries, Tadatoshi Akiba was active in the anti-nuclear movement, a movement that suffered a bitter factional split in 1963. That schism is the focus of the opening chapter of *Hiroshima Notes* by Kenzaburo Oe, published in 1965 (an English translation became available in 1981), a collection of essays about "the human face visible in and through all the death, desolation and suffering wrought in Hiroshima." Oe writes of the heros of Hiroshima, people who "refused to surrender to the worst despair or to incurable madness," people of genuine resolve and courage.

> If we ever experience another massive nuclear flash and thunder over our heads again, I am sure that the morality for survival when surrounded by death and desolation will need to draw on the wisdom of those who, through their bitter experience of Hiroshima, became the first moralists, "interpreters of human nature," in our nuclear age.

Of *Hiroshima Notes*, Dr. Akiba writes that it "gave expression to thoughts that I had not been able to put into words, to emotions that would only have been betrayed by clumsy expressions. It gave its readers hope and a new perspective." That perspective—the human cost of the bomb—became the focus of the Hibakusha Travel Grant Program that Dr. Akiba established in 1979, while a professor at Tufts University. The project sends a small number of journalists each year to Hiroshima and Nagasaki. With the assistance of vol-

Those Who Hunger and Thirst for Justice

unteer interpreters who "convey the deep feelings of hibakusha. . . of their decades of suffering and subsequent awakening to their mission," reporters function as communicators across the barriers of cultural misconceptions.

While working on this and other projects Dr. Akiba met a variety of peace activists, and participants in the nuclear freeze movement. He found it distressing that there was "little sign that American society as a whole has consciously re-evaluated its judgment on the righteousness of the bombing of Hiroshima and Nagasaki." Even among activists he found a self-centeredness, with a focus on "how 'I' can survive an all-out nuclear war," not a sense of responsibility for the arsenal of nuclear weapons this country possesses. This attitude contrasts with that of hibakusha who have said for forty years that, "We have lived through this hell and we don't want anyone else to ever have to live through it again." Dr. Akiba attributes this altruism to the teachings of Shinran (1173-1262), a great Buddhist of the middle ages:

> The attitudes of hibakusha are a manifestation of the Vow of Amida Buddha. Amida decides not to accept salvation, although he is in a position to be saved, unless all others are saved as well. He even returns from that world to this in order to use the understanding he gained for this purpose. The resemblance of Amida's behavior and hibakusha's behavior impressed me a great deal. In one count,

Rachelle Linner

90% of Hiroshima hibakusha are members of the sect initiated by Shinran. It is not surprising that, having had one of the worst experiences in the history of humanity, they relied on their religion to help them live through the awful suffering.

Buddhist Hiroshima and Christian Nagasaki responded differently to the bombings they experienced, a difference that is summarized in the phrase ''the rage of Hiroshima and the prayers of Nagasaki.'' The religious sensibility Dr. Akiba describes is companionable with that of Christian Nagasaki, a city whose faith has been intricately bound to experiences of martyrdom.

Dr. Akiba notes that ''feelings are very much determined by culture and experience and cannot be readily shared,'' a situation complicated in this case by the painful fact of racism in the historical relationship of Japan and the United States. (John Dower, a professor of Japanese studies at the University of California in San Diego, has written an important study of the role of race in the Pacific War. *War Without Mercy*, which received the 1986 National Book Critics Circle Award, draws on Japanese and American songs, slogans, cartoons, propaganda and other documents of the time. It is a powerful and convincing work.)

Westerners, because of a shared Christian vocabulary, may more easily understand the writing of Takashi Nagai, M.D. A hibakusha from Nagasaki, his book

Those Who Hunger and Thirst for Justice

The Bells of Nagasaki is subtitled "A Message of Hope From a Witness, A Doctor." A diary of medical relief efforts after the bombing, *The Bells of Nagasaki* is a powerful meditation about redemptive suffering. "...the people of Nagasaki confront the world and cry out: No more war! Let us follow the commandment of love and work together. The people of Nagasaki prostrate themselves before God and pray: Grant that Nagasaki may be the last atomic wilderness in the history of the world."

Thirty-seven at the time of the bombing, Dr. Nagai and his wife, Midori (a devout Christian, a child of martyrs) were the parents of two children. He served as Dean of the Department of Radiology at the University of Nagasaki Medical School. Dr. Nagai was injured by the blast, yet was instrumental in caring for other victims. He offers a description of the most basic relief efforts because what was needed most, a sophisticated medical delivery system, had been decimated of personnel and supplies.

Dr. Nagai's loss is outlined in the book's introduction, written by the translator, William Johnston, S.J.:

> He has lost his beloved wife, his house, his possessions, his health. He has seen his people by the thousands torn and lacerated by atomic wounds. He has seen the destruction of Japanese cities, the collapse of the Japan he loved, the failure of the ideology to which he dedicated his life.

Rachelle Linner

He has seen the cruel humiliation of his country, culminating in the surrender on the battleship *Missouri* and the American occupation of Japan. And now he lies dying, knowing that his children will be orphans.

And through this suffering a new and prophetic Nagai is born. Previously he was passionately devoted to the sick as part of the Japanese war effort; now he is passionately devoted to the sick because they are human beings. Previously he was devoted to victory for Japan; now he is devoted to world peace. He still loves his country; but now he is committed to the spiritual reconstruction of a Japan that will work for world peace. His whole life is centered on the greatest commandment, the commandment of love.

And as such, Father Johnston asserts, Dr. Nagai is a model of conversion to authentic religion, a conversion

> . . . of heart and mind, based on profound enlightenment, on revolution in consciousness. It transforms the whole person; it transforms the unconscious; and when a significant number of people are converted it transforms the collective unconscious. In the modern world this transformation will only be authentic if it brings us to love our neighbor and to a radical commitment to world peace.

Kokura, not Nagasaki, was the intended target of the second bomb, a fact that Dr. Nagai refers to in his "Funeral Address for the Victims of the Atomic Bomb."

Those Who Hunger and Thirst for Justice

But since the sky over that city was covered with clouds, the American pilots found it impossible to aim at their target. Consequently, they suddenly changed their plans and decided to drop the bomb on Nagasaki, the secondary target. However, yet another hitch occurred. As the bomb fell, cloud and wind carried it slightly north of the munitions factories over which it was supposed to explode, and it exploded over the cathedral. This is what I have heard. If it is true, the American pilots did not aim at Urakami [The Catholic district of Nagasaki]. It was the providence of God that carried the bomb to that destination.

Dr. Nagai believed that Nagasaki was chosen ''as a victim, a pure lamb, to be slaughtered and burned on the altar of sacrifice to expiate the sins committed by humanity in the Second World War. . . . in order to restore peace in the world it was not sufficient to repent. We had to obtain God's pardon through the offering of a great sacrifice.''

In the burden of the Potsdam Declaration is the ''painful path'' which is also ''the path of hope which gives to us sinners an opportunity to expiate our sins.''

Blessed are those that mourn for they shall be comforted. We must walk this way of expiation faithfully and sincerely. And as we walk in hunger and thirst, ridiculed, penalized, scourged, pouring with sweat and covered with blood, let us remember Jesus Christ who carried His cross to the hill of Calvary. He will give us courage.

Rachelle Linner

Before his death from leukemia in 1951 Dr. Nagai was a significant spokesman for Nagasaki hibakusha. His writings remain in print. In Japan some observers have been critical of a theology that would see the atomic bombings as an act of God. This theology was addressed by Pope John Paul II who, in 1981, became the first pontiff to visit Hiroshima and Nagasaki. Over and over he declared that war is an act of man, not God.

The power of Dr. Nagai's vision is that he sees a loving Providence in a dark time of history, and because of that human pain is elevated to share in that of Christ on the cross, a crucifixion that led to resurrection. "We can weep with the bones of our dead," Dr. Nagai wrote, "but we should struggle on."

> Though it may not be apparent to the eye, the atomic desert is gradually sending forth new shoots of life. Living with deep faith and enduring courageously, this tiny group of people, who know the happiness of weeping, is suffering to make amends for the sins of the world.

Completed in 1946, *The Bells of Nagasaki* was not published until 1949, after extensive negotiations with Occupation censors, who insisted an appendix be included that listed Japanese war crimes in the Phillipines (thus, at least implicitly, acknowledging that is what the atomic bombings were). The Press Code, issued on September 19, 1945, was "designed to educate the press of the Japanese in the responsibilities and meaning of a free press'' and became, in effect, blanket censorship over ''news, editorials and advertisements of all newspapers and will cover, in addition, all publications printed in Japan.'' The Press Code insured that ''there shall be no destructive criticism of the Allied Forces of Occupation and nothing which might invite mistrust or resentment of those troops.'' It proscribed the printing of anything ''which might, directly or by inference, disturb the public tranquility.'' Certainly early works of hibakusha testimony were affected by the Press Code; despite this, many notable collections of personal accounts exist, written with immediacy and power. Unfortunately comparatively few are available in English. Once the Occupation ended hibakusha writings became increasingly anti-nuclear; a perspective echoed in the strong Japanese response to the 1954 *Lucky Dragon* incident. The crew and cargo of a Japanese tuna-fishing vessel, with the ironic name of *Lucky Dragon Number Five,* was contaminated by radioactive fallout from the testing of American hydrogen weapons tess at the Bikini Atoll. One crew member died.

By erecting a barrier against learning the true dimensions of the suffering that results from atomic attack, the Press Code set the pattern for what still continues today as the secrecy and duplicity of governments in acknowledging the dangers of radiation.

Rachelle Linner

The city of Hiroshima has extended honorary citizenship to three Americans: Norman Cousins (for his work with the Moral Adoption Movement and the Hiroshima Maidens), Floyd Schmoe (who raised funds in the United States and built homes for hibakusha) and Barbara Reyonlds, a woman whose peace witness and support for hibakusha led her on a spritual pilgrimage she writes of with simple eloquence. Her insights illumine the dimensions of Hiroshima's gift to the world.

Barbara and Earl Reynolds and their three children went to Hiroshima in 1951. Earl, an anthropologist, was appointed to the staff of the Atomic Bomb Casualty Commission (ABCC). (Established in 1947 to study the delayed effects of radiation exposure, ABCC was a research and diagnostic, rather than treatment facility. Some of its practices, most notably an aggressive autopsy program, fostered hibakusha's sense that they were used as guinea pigs. The U.S.-sponsored ABCC was dissolved in 1975 and replaced with the joint U.S.-Japan Radiation Effects Research Foundation, RERF.)

Living fifteen miles from Hiroshima the Reynolds' knew little about hibakusha.

Most of our information and impressions came from the families who lived with us on the American base and from the American colleagues with whom my husband worked. Many of these had been there only a few months longer than we ourselves yet they spoke with authority.

90

Those Who Hunger and Thirst for Justice

('You rarely see anyone that's scarred or maimed.' 'The effects are greatly overrated...' 'No genetic effects...' 'They only want to forget the whole thing.') We believed because we wanted to believe.

(That process, of believing what we want to believe, continues to prevail in regard to Hiroshima. Some people think that nuclear war is survivable, arguing that Hiroshima and Nagasaki rebuilt—what they do not mention is that the two cities, as grievously as they suffered, received help from an intact society around them. And the weapons used against them were primitive compared to those we possess today.)

In 1954 the Reynolds' embarked on a unique journey on a yacht they had built. For three years they and the three young crewmen from Hiroshima traveled around the world. At each port they stopped at the Japanese crew was questioned about the bomb and its effect. Ironically that is how this American family learned about the true dimensions of Hiroshima's suffering, and heard too the fears and anger of people who could only glimpse the terror that was now part of the world.

Returning from Hawaii to Hiroshima in 1958, the Reynolds were arrested for sailing into the American nuclear test zone in the Pacific, a protest that resulted in Earl Reynolds' arrest. Acquitted after two years of trials and appeals, they finally returned to Hiroshima to listen to hibakusha, and learn.

Rachelle Linner

I began to learn about the unpredictable, sobering, and never-ending effects of the atomic bomb. And it was then that I came into contact with the hibakusha's unique and consuming desire for a world without war. They alone had experienced what it will be like if we fail to move beyond war.

The hibakusha alone have no conflict of interest. Their consuming desire is for a world without war for they have seen the end of that road with the resultant destruction of the world—their world. They continue to say, as with a single voice, 'We do not accept the manufacture, testing, or stock-piling of nuclear weapons by any nation anywhere, for any purpose whatsoever.'

In the years following their return the Reynolds' worked with hibakusha to spread their message of peace. This work included peace missions that toured many nations and solitary prayer vigils at the Cenotaph. Yet there was personal pain in the midst of this work; the Reynolds' divorced in 1965 and Barbara Reynolds found herself "alone, discredited and broke." From the darkness she was drawn to the witness of "faith-filled" people like Dr. Takuo Matsumoto, a hibakusha who, in 1965, was 77.

How had he been able to remain so serene...radiating forgiveness and love? He had been president of the Girl's Mission School in Hiroshima when the atomic bomb fell, killing more than 350 of the junior high students, eigh-

Those Who Hunger and Thirst for Justice

teen teachers—and his own wife. Yet he had not turned against God.

She sees in him witness to "total submission to a God who was both merciful and just, the God whom Jesus made known." She prayed for faith.

> I do believe that the 'Inward Light' is Jesus Christ and that He is there, waiting to be recognized and received by each person, of whatever religion, who hungers and thirsts after righteousness and seeks to live out your law of love. Help me to know Him better and to follow wherever He may lead.

"Light, like a sunrise, dispelled the darkness."

> I, who had lost so much only to be given everything, was able to share my joy and my faith with others who had lost everything—even hope—yet who came to comfort me....I found myself surrounded by evidences of God's caring. I knew then that God had a mighty plan for Hiroshima and Nagasaki...and for hibakusha, whom He loves with a very special love—just as He has a plan for His Church, and for me, and for all who, turning away from reliance on weapons or war, will trust in Him alone.

The fruits of Mrs. Reynolds' conversion are visible in the World Friendship Center, which she established in 1965 ("a place where people from many countries can bring their fears and their guilt and their discouragement and find a warming fire burning into which they can cast their despair and from which they can light a torch of hope'') and at the Hiroshima/Nagasaki Memorial Collection at Wilmington College in Wilmington, Ohio. She has continued to share the way hibakusha have lived their years of atomic suffering, ''a gentle way, a loving way, a way that somehow trusts the goodness in all people and seeks to speak to that.'' And for people trapped in a sense of powerlessness in the face of the nuclear threat Barbara Reynolds has become a ''faith-filled'' witness, honoring hibakusha and allowing people to learn of their ''gentle way,'' extending with deep generosity a spiritual hospitality to those who hesitate.

Susumu Ishitani experienced the bomb in Nagasaki. He was thirteen at the time. A third generation Christian, Dr. Ishitani writes of an encounter he had, soon after the war, with an American conscientious objector.

I was shocked and deeply impressed when I met a man from America who said he had been a conscientious objector during the war and came to Japan immediately after the war to help the Japanese people who were in trouble. I had never heard before that there was such a thing as a C.O. existing anywhere in the world. He told us how he got into trouble with his own parents and the community around his family due to his commitment and how he lost one of his kidneys cooperating in a medical experiment in which he was used as a guinea pig.

As I heard him and spent some time with him, I had a firm conviction that this person was showing a real way for Christians to live in present society. I was then an eleventh grader....I held a firm conviction that I was a child of God rather than a Japanese and a human being rather than a member of a nation; I should have more loyalty to God and humanity.

...when it is necessary I need to be able to behave like Jesus Christ who lived and died for the benefit of other human beings and for the glory of the divine. Therefore I have to make the place where I was born and where I live a place suitable to that end.

Nagasaki *has* been the last atomic wilderness in the world, and who is not to say it is because of the way hibakusha have lived? They have been pilgrims, wandering the world to bear witness to atomic war. Look at us, they say. We have seen people suffer and die and we cannot begin to describe what we saw. We do not want anyone else to suffer as we have. Look at us. Our bone and marrow has been invaded by radiation, our skin burned with a heat so intense that it melted. Look at us. Imagine the memories of pain we hold in our hearts. Look at us and know that the time of nation-states is over: we are one community with one destiny. We share the same fate.

Rachelle Linner

The people in these pages are diverse, speaking from different religious traditions, different nations, but each incarnate a way of being that stands in opposition to the idolatry of the nuclear age. In religious terms they are prophets who challenge our hardness of heart: we who worship idols have become like them with ears that hear not and eyes that do not see. Hibakusha, who saw the burning flesh and heard the pleas for water, have given us the time to turn our hearts away from that idolatry.

Let us prostrate ourselves before God and pray: Grant that Nagasaki may be the last atomic wilderness in the history of the world.

The Merciful

Patrick Jordan

IN THE north portico of the cathedral of Chartres there is a remarkable image of Christ in stone, a cross in relief in the halo behind his head. He is erect but slightly bent over a blind man. Perhaps the blind man is the one from John's Gospel, born that way, the one Jesus cured by making a paste of mud and spit and putting it on the man's eyes. Jesus' two cupped hands engulf the man's tilted head. Large and sure, they seem to be infusing light.

The hands are not those of a technician, antiseptically and mathematically correct, infinitely removed. Nor are they flawed by the least hint of sentiment. They are the hands of one who knows affliction, the hands of one who has created darkness and light

Of course, in point of fact, this representation from Chartres is not Jesus healing the blind man at all. It is, as the other side of a photo card sent me attests, *Dieu creant Adam.* It was I who had misperceived and miscast the whole thing. But revelation comes like that. I had not expected the Creator to look so young, so

Patrick Jordan

engaged, so full of energy, presence and compassion, so Christ-like. It was my eyes that had to be opened.

In Hebrew, God is referred to as *Ay ha-rehamin*, the Father of Mercy. His loving-kindness, his *hesed*, creates, delivers and sustains. In point of fact, this *hesed* is the ultimate key to understanding God's character. As John McKenzie writes, the entire history of God's dealings with Israel can be summed up as *hesed*: the covenant is *hesed*, a preservation of *hesed*, a demonstration of it. And the consequence is that God expects active *hesed* of Israel, within itself, and also toward outsiders. *Hesed* is thus the *imitatio dei* and the fulfillment of the Law. As parable, it is Jesus; Samaritan.

I first learned of St. Rose's Home for incurable cancer patients on Manhattan's Lower East Side from Dorothy Day. After leaving the Catholic Worker, I spent nearly seven years there as a nursing assistant. I came to know hundreds of dying women and men over the years. Many I cannot forget.

One of these had grown up in that very Cherry Street neighborhood over sixty years before. He looked utterly terrified when he first arrived at St. Rose's from the big C. hospital uptown, and took his place in the four-bed ward. He told me that, as a Jewish kid in the neighborhood, he had avoided going anywhere near St. Rose's. He said distinctly that it was known by all the kids as "the bones house."

The man was full of nervous humor, quick of mind,

The Merciful

and had robust-looking skin. But the latter was, a veneer, top skin only, the color a side effect of some chemical endeavor by the doctors uptown. The veneer was the final high-tide mark they had left him. For the rest, they had now given up on him. And so it was with his humor. Beneath its quickness and wit was the cry of a dispirited man, as paralyzed as his own body.

Not long after he died at St. Rose's (a peaceful death months after his frenetic arrival), his blood brother came and eventually left the same way. I can remember them, and many others, some conquering, and some failing to come to terms with the fears of childhood.

The house of bones. It stands, preserved each day by the Offertory prayer of one of the Dominican sisters for ''protection against fire and disaster,'' next to the East River, separating Manhattan from Brooklyn. By the time I arrived, it was not the 1800s row house Nathaniel Hawthorne's daughter Rose Lathrop had turned into her first hospice for indigent cancer victims at the turn of the century, but was a sturdy, efficient building, six stories high, from the prosperous fifties. One visitor, coming to spend time with a dying friend, recalled with a start having driven the piles for the building's foundations. He hadn't known what the site was going to be, and this was the first time he had returned to the neighborhood in twenty years. His discovery was the best gift he felt he could have given his friend.

Patrick Jordan

The FDR Drive, one of the chief north-south arteries of the city, lies between St. Rose's and the river. Across the river lies the Brooklyn Navy Yard, or what remains of it—a few huge ships at a time are still remantled there. One patient—gangly, gray and whispering with want of oxygen—pointed over at its skeletal cranes: "I know where I got this," and he motioned to his chest. He had sprayed ships there with asbestos during the war. Now the fires he had prevented on shipboard had all come to burn in his chest.

There were hundreds of people who died at St. Rose's during the years I worked there. Hundreds, but the place was never a house of bones. Even for the trembling brothers, it was finally something more, closer to a haven than a dead end, a place where a hand might take yours. Quickly enough, and often enough, that is what the dying and their people came to feel. The morticians said as much. There is a special character to any such place, dependent entirely on its people. It is rooted in those who founded it, but continues to be formed by those carrying it on now, and of course by those who die there. While St. Rose's is clearly an institution, caring for about forty dying people at any given time, there is nonetheless a marked graciousness atypical of large places. Rose Lathrop had said to keep it small. There was the presence of color and light, an uncommon cleanliness, and a taste for often doing things with a special touch. On St. Nicholas Day, a mythical bishop visited each person to present gifts.

The Merciful

But it was more often a daily matter. A mortician once told me as we made the trip to his waiting hearse: ''You could blindfold me and I would know this was St. Rose's. There isn't another morgue like it in the city of New York.'' Care is like that, like the sculptures of Chartres: a mercy extended over time.

Baron von Hugel wrote that there is no humility without humiliation, and Orwell that ''natural death, almost by definition, means something slow, smelly, and painful.'' The lame, the halt, and the blind; the deaf, the stroke-ridden, the aphasic, the comatose, the forsaken, the homeless: they all came to St. Rose's in cancer's throes. Even there, they would each one suffer further forms of humiliation. The international banker, the nun, the missionary, the lawyer, the doctor, the convicted murderer, the boat refugee, the undocumented alien, the baker: each one was brought even lower sooner than she or he had reckoned.

All came, all were welcomed, but none was spared. Each had unique tears, pains, and smells, a brace of what Teilhard termed ''passive diminishments'' to scourge the heart. For all the care, for all the solicitude of those who had loved ones, this was still finally the Way of the Cross and the lamb's bones were left broken. It was as if the Mother Superior in Poulenc's *Dialogues of the Carmelites* was saying again and again: ''What God desires to test is not your strength but your weakness.''

Ah, what pitiful mouths some, fighting for the breath

that even the oxygen machines could not bring enough of. Some were veritable engines, pumping up torrents of purulent fluid. Their abdomens swelled like whales, so high they could no longer see or eventually remember their toes. Each tapping spelled more limited success and a diminished amount of time before the process needed to be repeated. The confused had to be restrained. Others would not open their mouths for fear of their own smell. And most shaming of all, the incontinence, the utter humiliation of loss of control before strangers.

I saw wounds that went to the bone: patients from the back wards of famous hospitals who arrived with fist-sized caverns to the spine. There were the gangrenous limbs and that pall of yellow that extends to every crevice of the dying liver patient. I saw growths that appear like volcanoes, red and blue mushrooms that erupted from the depths of the forest. I saw holes where they shouldn't have been, fissures that connected the wrong channels, eyes that were not there, skin that tore at the touch. But worst of all, I saw death by a word: a long-time patient who was snubbed by another long-timer (they had seen and survived many deaths together), simply took to his bed from the slight, opened not his mouth again—for food, water or words—and died.

Dying is like being born: inevitably painful and unique in duration. Some final agonies were not three

The Merciful

hours but three months. They could have convinced even an agnostic of the death-defying potential of life. What some endured was terrifying.

Jesus went to the tomb of Lazarus and wept. He touched the widow's son and returned him to life. But all these died. And when Ivan Ilych heard the death rattle from his own throat in Tolstoy's tale, and those around him saying, "It is finished," he still had the presence to repeat the words in his own soul. He not only heard them, but held and heeded them. And then there was light.

What can one possibly do in a cancer ward, an AIDS hospital, an Alzheimer's asylum to turn the tide? One can only not withhold oneself. One must reach out to the *agnus dei* being broken there. It happens in the small things primarily. To be faithful in great measures, be faithful in the little ones. "We must speak to them with our hands before we speak to them with our lips," Peter Claver said on tending the slaves from the chattel ships in the early 1600s.

At St. Rose's that effort began with the whirlpool bath, the bath of immersion. If the person was strong enough, she or he was lowered, if need be on a sling, into the large tub. There, with special soaps in the warm, swirling water, ages were sometimes removed, the bitter taste of some hospital experiences excised. There were medicated shampoos for severe skin disorders. If a person could not leave bed, a contoured trough was placed under the head and the shampoo rinsed into a bucket. Men were shaved; nails, horn-like, clipped; glasses cleansed; wax extracted; pain medications regulated and heightened to need. Beds were specialized with air mattresses, down, sheepskin, water mattresses or thermal blankets. When the sheets weighed too heavily and lay like chains, they were tented up. Limp limbs were positioned on pillows. There were the recommended turnings.

I can remember removing layers of dead skin from feet that looked like heavy yellow squash, bathing them repeatedly, using oil, scraping off what had not been cared for in memory. I remember coming to realize that each toe is distinct in all creation, that the folds of skin in the human body are a map as variegated as the earth's surface. I came to realize the sacramental nature of turning and touch, of feeding in drops, of taking more time than seemed available, or warming one's own hands on a cold morning so as not to startle, of approaching the deaf and the blind as if one were in the presence of the mystical hind.

I remember the night watches, suctioning the same individual a dozen times—the bottles of the Gumco machine filling up like a sump pump—and his eyes and his hand reaching to say thank you. I can remember when the dawn would finally break over the river. If the wards had slept peacefully, the words of Zechariah would slowly come to mind: the loving-kindness, the

The Merciful

hesed of God, had again visited us like the dawn from on high, guiding us in the shadow of death and our feet into the way of peace.

All these matters were simply techniques taught in nursing-care 1A. There was clearly nothing heroic about them. But their execution today is sadly and too often the exception. Ask most nurses if they are allowed to provide the care they would wish to give, in fact were trained to give. As Solzhenitsyn's *Cancer Ward* ably portrayed, it is the modern bureaucratic institution, inhumanely directed to itself and to the bottom line, that is more deadly to the human spirit than cancer itself. We need to hear St. Paul, that acts of mercy must be done with cheerfulness.

I can remember a ninety-seven-year-old man, nearly blind and unable to move from his bed, who wanted to play a piano again. Perhaps he had heard of Casals at that age. A piano was finally brought up to the floor and moved next to his bed. The professor, for that he was (emeritus to spare) from Columbia Law School in near pre-Columbian times, was lifted to the piano chair. It was like seeing Casals himself, bent over his keyboard to play Bach each morning as a benediction on the day, his hands gathering strength as he played and his body righting with the notes. So it was and so it happened with this man.

Come to the waters and drink freely. St. Rose's, as does Mother Teresa, welcomes each one without charge. It is an act of faith. Rose Lathrop had said: accept no government money. And so it is still done. Free-will offerings only, from those inspired by the work. From the patients and their families, not a cent, not a Medicaid or insurance card. All blue shields are laid down at the door, and Sisyphus' stone is finally pushed to the side. In their dying hours, some finally make it home free for the first time.

Mercy is like that, like the tides in the East River, mercy, upon mercy, upon mercy. I and many others experienced it at St. Rose's. It goes on there today, and in a thousand other places, more hidden and more blessed still.

Suffering is the gate to paradise. How we go through it is left to us. I shall never forget Bernie. He was young and powerful, but he was paralyzed and speechless. There came a point when he had to be suctioned nearly constantly. The last time there came forth a profusion of liquid, but nothing alarming. But the alarms went off soon enough.

Bernie suddenly started vomiting mouthfulls of blood, projected onto the sheets, the bed, over part of the room. All was done that could be to stop the hemorrhaging—positioning, the proper medical personnel, medicated injections. But it was all too clear that it was too late: even in a cancer ward, death comes thievingly. In these hardest cases there still remains nothing but prayer and fasting. We started to pray fast:

the rosary in the hour of death, a circle around his bed. I remember taking Bernie's hand and holding him. I felt a terrible responsibility. Without the suctioning would he have lived longer? But that was in God's hands. In the instant before his eyes lost their final register, in the instant after he had won the ultimate victory over his own terrifying fright, Bernie looked at me directly with a remarkable, even tender forgiveness. The man had found his very self, and I will take that moment to the grave. The final mercy was his.

"To the blood Our Lord will pour out, O Christian," goes an old French hymn, "add at least your tears." There will be many more occasions, for the blood of Christ is being poured out daily.

When Jesus faulted the Pharisees and called them whitewashed sepulchers, it was not over some pitiful, small-handed hypocrisy. It was for having neglected "the most important matters of the Law—justice, mercy and faithfulness." The three, like the social, personal and spiritual aspects of our own nature, cannot be separated. Each must be engaged: the cancerous structures of our societies which suck the blood from God's treasured ones (justice); the neighbor who requires each of us to walk the second mile (mercy); and the essential obligation of our being, the worship of God with our hands, hearts, and minds, and the love of others (faithfulness). To neglect any one of these weakens the others and diminishes the whole, the body of Christ.

There was in the Children's Museum of Los Angeles a room to which crowds of youngsters gravitated. It was covered throughout with photographic sheets. Periodically a flash would be set off, and as the light faded, the form of any shadow projected in the instant of exposure remained, for perhaps half a minute or more, on the room's walls and floor. The children were of course delighted. They saw what they had not expected—their own images, embossed briefly on the photographic field. Soon they were experimenting, turning their bodies into all sorts of exotic shadowy forms. And after each form had faded, the light would suddenly flash on again. Those who were prepared, would quickly fashion a new and more striking image.

Mercy is like that. It appears brightly in every age and renews the light. It is the image of the living God, bending over those blinded with an artisan's willing hands. It is a Rose Lathrop caring for cancer victims in one age; a family opening its home to those with AIDS in another; a parish offering respite care for those with Alzheimer's disease in another. In each, it is the living God giving that recognition we each restlessly crave. "This day," we are told, "you shall be with me in paradise." And in this kindness, this relationship, we at last taste that which is a greater good than life itself. We taste paradise already.

The Pure of Heart

Brendan J. Freeman

DID you ever meditate on a Japanese landscape painting? There is nothing photographic about it. Usually a few strokes of the brush represents a tree, a few lines, a meandering stream. Everything in the painting, though rooted in the earth, seems to float in empty space. I am told in fact that space is more important than form in these paintings. Space does not so much surround the scene, as the scene itself articulates the space. To me this gives the whole picture a feeling that there is more than meets the eye. The eye relaxes but the heart is somehow awakened to another dimension. Of course in the enigmatic way of Buddhist thinking, if you can describe that "other dimension" you have not really experienced it. But that is not the concern here.

I like to approach the scriptures in the same quiet way one approaches a Japanese print. The stories and parables of Jesus, for example, are never closed units. They open out into infinite space. They allow for a wide range of interpretation. Our Lord seldom stated the exact meaning of his words. His parables are not mathematical equations for good living nor formulas for problem solving, but rather they draw our hearts out of themselves into a new way of understanding our lives. His stories are deliberately incomplete. They await the inclusion of our lives. Each person fills in the blank space, with the details of his or her own life situation.

The eight sentences that make up the beatitudes have grown into a library of commentaries. This is as it should be because they are living words and one living word puts us in contact with countless other words.

The sixth beatitude, "Blessed are the pure of heart for they shall see God," is a mirror before which we stand to find our Christian identity. The first thing we notice when we stand before the mirror of scripture is that, unlike other mirrors, it reflects more than is put before it. Not only is our life reflected but the ultimate meaning of our life.

What question then should we bring to the mirror-like words, "Blessed are the pure of heart?" These words do not easily give themselves to us. Like the children in the gospel story, the music is playing but we have forgotten the dance. We hear and hear again but do not understand. The word heart, for instance, is one of the most important metaphors in the Bible, but to our minds the meaning of this word is often lost. Recently I was reading an article discussing political

The Pure of Heart

candidates. The author, in a few sentences, summed up the confusion surrounding the word heart. He writes: " According to recent polls what voters today most of all want in a President is to have Heart or Soul. Apparently the words are interchangeable, which is fitting, since they are equally meaningless—sort of linguistic grunts of the inarticulate." (*Reflections* by Richard Harris; *New Yorker* 8/3/87, p. 65).

Behind a statement like this lies a whole wasteland of lost words. To our modern ears, words that express the reality of our inner life seem like grunts of the inarticulate. Have we become so externalized, so out of touch with our spirit that words such as heart and soul are meaningless? These words are meant to have expressive power in our life. They are meant to awaken in us the reality they speak about. In his famous poem "The Second Coming," William Butler Yeats wrote:

Turning and turning in a widening gyre
the falcon cannot hear the falconer.

The widening gyre of modern life takes us away from our center. The words "Blessed are the pure of heart" can barely be heard in the press of life. They are words that call us back to the center of our being. The psalmist prayed: "A pure heart create for me O God, put a steadfast spirit within me." With all the good intentions in the world we find ourselves drifting away from our center. We experience the divisions in our heart. We are no stranger to anxiety, alienation, separation. These are experiences of the human predicament in our times. Rare is the person who does not go through some kind of breakdown. All of us search for our identity. Pain plays an important part in this search. Self-estrangement, self-alienation, the anxiety, complexity and stress of modern living are all painful experiences. But they are only painful because they presuppose an opposite situation: being one with ourselves, being at home with ourselves, establishing meaning and values that do not break down at the first challenge. To do this we have to find the center of our personal being. This does not mean once we find such a place all will be easy. No, we never really arrive once and for all at the center—we are always on the way. We have to know at least where to look and how to begin to return to ourselves.

There is an interesting story in the life of St. Benedict as told by St. Gregory. A group of monks asked Benedict to be their leader. He reluctantly agreed but after a very short time realized it would never work out. St. Gregory says of the monks, "they could not see why they should have to force their settled minds into new ways of thinking." St. Benedict knew he could not force them so he decided to leave. He went back to his hermitage to "live alone with himself in the presence of his heavenly Father."

The Pure of Heart

What does it mean to live with himself? Gregory answers, ''. . .great anxieties can carry us out of ourselves even though we still remain what we are; we are too busy with other matters to look into our souls.'' St. Gregory delves into this a little more deeply by recalling the example of the Prodigal son in Luke's gospel. After squandering his inheritance he was reduced to a swineherd. At a point of despair, the gospel says he ''came to himself'' and even though he was in a distant country he decided to make the long journey home to his father.

We can apply the images to our own lives. When we are not living in the presence of God we can be considered to be away from our true selves; in a distant and unfamiliar county. It seems to be a law of our nature that we, like the prodigal son, have to hit bottom before our hearts awaken and desire a better life. This awakening of our hearts, this coming to ourselves is the first step in conversion—a turning toward home. Each of us has an inventory of things that take us away from our true selves, from our center, and make us forgetful of our intimate relationship with God.

The journey home is very beautiful indeed. St. Teresa of Avila compares our heart to an interior castle. At the very center of this castle—which is the very center of our personal life—dwells Christ. The various rooms leading to the center are states of interior prayer. Before we can begin this journey to the center however, we have to desire to embark. If our hearts are asleep we will never know the journey. In a word, we have to know there is a journey to be made. In the first chapter of her book Teresa writes:

> Wouldn't it show great ignorance, my daughters, if someone when asked who he was didn't know? Well, now, if this would be so extremely stupid, we are incomparably more so when we do not strive to know who we are, but limit ourselves to considering roughly these bodies. Because we have heard and because faith tells us so, we know we have souls. But we seldom consider the precious things that can be found in the soul (*Interior Castle*, Ch. 1:2).

The words heart and soul are interchangeable; they express the deepest truth about our life. They are the words we use to express God—within us. I like to mentally picture myself sitting by a spring of water which feeds a brook. This spring apparently comes from some hidden place in the earth. To find our heart means to dwell at that place within us where God is pouring our life into us like a spring of water. Each moment of our existence God's life is flowing into us and sustaining us in being. We are, each minute, being made into the image and likeness of God. Scripture calls this place a "garden enclosed"—it is the place where the Holy Spirit gives words to our hearts desire—our place of prayer, our Garden of Eden. But we have been banished from the garden. The Genesis account of the banishment of Adam and Eve is our story also. We have been cast out and wander about the earth separated from our source, forgetful of who we really are, yet never entirely forgetful. There is always a little flame of desire for our homeland, a little flicker of memory calling us to return.

The scriptures and the writings of the spiritual masters have outlined the return journey for us. The path is steep and the way narrow that leads to our heart but we will never rest until we find the way. Our restless hearts are really our first guides because they tell us something is amiss. What a shame to bury this pain under layer after layer of distractions and amusements and escapes. The real climate in which our hearts awaken is empty space. The very emptiness of our lives is speaking to us. The desert drew the ancient monks into its overflowing silence and their main occupation was to wait, to do nothing but let God come to life in them. Then their heart would find voice and pray—then they would become fully human.

We, of course, cannot live that way but we must allow ourselves to feel emptiness, to have patience and be watchful. Our heart will find voice only if we give it space. Millions of dollars are spent every day just to fill the empty places of our life with trivial amusements. Did you ever stop to think how much time, energy and money are spent just to provide comfort

Brendan J. Freeman

for ourselves, to distract us and give us instant relief from whatever bothers us? We are lulled into a world of unreality.

One author, Ann Schaef, in her work *Co-Dependence*, claims the majority of our society is addicted to some form of compulsive behavior. Either alcohol, drugs, food, work, relationships or a whole host of other disorders that we use to keep us free from facing the pain of being separated from the source and origin of our life.

This is what the monastic fathers would call the land of forgetfulness or the sleep of the soul. In our day, according to Paul Tillich, existentialist authors and artists have provided the context in which the Christian message of salvation can be most effectively preached. They have almost brutally uncovered the artificiality of much of our modern culture. Accordingly there is "no escape" from the human condition. There is "no exit." Yet it is just this predicament that the gospel addresses. The fathers of the church and of monasticism who understood the problems of their times were very successful in bringing the "good news" of redemption to the "no escape" situations of the people for whom they wrote.

Tillich mentions that it was the monastic authors of the Middle Ages who were the forerunners of the existentialists. Within their communities they analyzed the human condition of estrangement, of life away

The Pure of Heart

from our source and origin. When this one primary relationship is foiled every other relationship is affected. One such author was William of St. Thierry, the great friend and biographer of St. Bernard. He describes what Heidegger calls "forgetfulness of being," as a sleep of the soul:

> I have learned to sleep with the sunshine full on my face and have grown used to it. I have become accustomed to not seeing what takes place before my eyes and, dead at heart as I am, though I am set in the midst of the sea, I have ceased to hear the roaring of the waves and the thunder of the sky (*Meditations* 2:4).

If we accept things just as they are without the use of our critical faculties then the whole inner life is lost to us. The sun is shining but we are in the dark. God's creative life is all around us but we do not see it. There is a place in our life where we receive our very breath, our very being and existence from God. It is a place where we know and speak to God as our Father. We call that place our heart, the center of our being and at that center we are continually conversing with God in prayer, whether we are aware of it or not.

St. Paul says the Holy Spirit is always praying in us. From the depth of our being to the depth of God's being there is an intimate love relationship. As we develop in life we should be growing in awareness of this continual prayer. It is as natural to us as breathing but we have to give time to it and wait in patience, always wait in patience. While we are often "away from ourselves" our truest desire is to be by that stream of prayer where the Father and Son and Holy Spirit converse with our spirit. To arrive at this place, of the interior castle as Teresa calls it, this still point of our being, we have to awaken to the fact that we are away from it. This awakening is the call of conversion. To experience the restlessness of life, as our heart increases its desire to dwell at the source, is the first awakening of our heart.

The second awakening is when we realize the true condition of our life when we stand before the words "Blessed are the *pure* of heart." This word pure, even more so than the word heart, can be harder to understand. Perhaps the translation in the New American Bible can help us here. They translate the word pure as single: "Blessed are the single-hearted...." But even here if we stand before the mirror and ask ourselves if we are single-hearted, we have to acknowledge that we are not. A pure heart is one in which there is no dross, no conflicting mixture of desires and passions. It is a state of rest and inner peace. The monastic fathers called this state "apatheia." This stillness within allows our heart to pray. A person with an undivided heart possesses a basic calmness even in the midst of turmoil. Even though we know we may never attain such an equanimity in our life, still to strive for tranquility within is important to prayer.

All of us have many demands and obligations, many conflicting drives and forces pulling us in every direction. As Paul says, "What we want to do, we can't do and what we don't want to do, we do." The peace of an undivided heart is achieved only after much discipline and training. The positive side of many of our works of penance and renunciation is that it quiets the conflict within. No matter which way you look at it, the seven capital sins still wreak havoc in our life. Self-denial in the traditional sense was meant to liberate us from the tyranny of our passions. Like so many other things in our Catholic past, penance and self-denial were separated from their main purpose and stood isolated, as if self-denial was a good in itself.

Part of the renewal in the spiritual life of the church is to see the inter-relatedness of all the works of asceticism handed down to us by tradition. A life of asceticism and discipline leads to harmony and inner peace. When the forces and drives in our life are in harmony we have a oneness with everything around us. Our inner and outer worlds are unified. Perhaps what the fathers called "apatheia" we would call integration.

The scriptures speak of this peaceful state in figurative language. "Heart" and "hand" denote the whole person. The heart signifies the inner life and the hands the outer action. In Psalm 25 the Psalmist asks who will stand in God's holy place. The answer is the person with "clean hands and pure heart." This is the person who puts into practice with his actions the good desires of his heart. I do not think we have to examine ourselves very closely to see where we stand in this regard. How often our good intentions die on the vine, never to become the fine wine of good works. We struggle, sometimes intensely, just to keep our evil desires at bay.

Struggle we will, but the important point here is that we honestly acknowledge our human condition. If the first step is finding our heart by identifying the source of pain in our life, and realizing how far we are from our true center, then the second step is to awaken our heart by honestly acknowledging what brought us so far from home. It is not easy to correctly name our sin. To do so is to pierce our heart—to open it to God's healing love. The root meaning of the word compunction is to pierce or puncture. This is what we do when we let the truth break into our life—we puncture the hard crust of sin surrounding our heart. Sin in our life does harden us, whereas true and abiding sorrow for sin softens our heart and leads to compassion.

St. Benedict, in his Rule for Monks, outlines twelve stages of spiritual growth. The twelfth and last stage is what we might call final integration. He says of a monk in this stage that he "not only has humility in

The Pure of Heart

his heart but his very appearance makes it manifest to those who see him'' (Ch. 7:62). Benedict then makes reference to the Gospel story of the two men who went up to the temple to pray. One a tax collector, the other a Pharisee. The Pharisee prayed in a very bragging, self-righteous way. He recounted to God all his so-called good works. The tax collector, on the other hand, would not even lift his eyes to heaven, but beat his breast, saying ''God, be merciful to me a sinner'' (Lk 18:13).

The story concludes by saying the prayer of the Pharisee, who was a professional religious, was not acceptable to God. God sees beyond the good works into the inner motivation of the heart. The tax collector who was commonly believed to be a public sinner, because of the truth in his heart, was acceptable to God.

If we examine the story we see the Pharisee did not bring his whole self to prayer. He left behind what he was ashamed of—the more undesirable part of himself. Yet it was this part of humanity that Jesus came to save. ''The healthy do not need a physician, but the sick.'' If we hide our ''sin-sickness'' from the Lord we miss the whole point of salvation. The Pharisee tried, like Adam and Eve, to hide from God, but instead of the shelter and thickets of the garden, he used his so-called good works as a camouflage. It is said that if we lie enough we end up believing the lie ourselves. The Pharisee, so out of touch with himself, easily fell into condemning others. He projected whatever evil was in his own heart onto the tax collector praying next to him. Judging and condemning others is the fruit that grows in the soil of self-illusion. The fruit of true prayer and self-knowledge is compassion for others.

The tax collector was deeply aware and in touch with his human condition. He took an entirely different approach to prayer than the Pharisee. He owned and acknowledged his sin. One of the basic truths about us is that we are sinners. To bypass this fact starts us off in the wrong direction. To run from it vitiates any attempt at prayer. True prayer springs almost naturally from a contrite heart. The tax-collector did not criticize or condemn others but simply and honestly stood before God and striking his breast—a symbol of a pierced heart—asked for mercy. Even though he might have been in a crowded temple he did not drag the failings of others into his relationship with God. He stood alone before God. Each of us has to stand in that same place. Alone before God. We only harm ourselves if we try to avoid being fully alone, because it is there that the merits of Jesus are given to us.

Denial of the truth of our aloneness before God is probably one of the biggest obstacles to being single-hearted or pure of heart. Psalm 51, *the* great prayer of contrition in the Bible, says God loves ''truth in the heart.'' We deceive ourselves when we only own the good things in our life and fail to look deeply into the dark side of our heart. There is a ''saying'' of the desert fathers to the effect that the one who knows his sin is greater than the one who raises the dead.

It is certainly rare for someone to have power over the grave—but even rarer to find someone who enters into the depths of sin. Only Jesus entered fully into that state—that experience of estrangement from God. We are called to stand before the mirror of God's great purity in all honesty. If we bring only what we consider our self-justifying good works we will never see in that mirror the meaning of mercy. We will miss the whole point of what it means to be redeemed by Christ. The experience of redemption can only come to those who have some taste of what it is to be unredeemed—a sinner—alone before God. Self-deception keeps us from experiencing our true identity. Self-knowledge puts truth in our heart and allows us to find our identity in God. This is self-knowledge with an awareness of our separation from God.

St. Bernard makes this type of knowledge the foundation of the spiritual life. Just before he died, Bernard completed a series of long letters to the Cistercian pope, Eugene III. To help Eugene stay rooted in his fundamental vocation as a monk, he exhorts him to never lose sight of who he is when every accidental is stripped away. He writes: "Now when you ask who you are, the response will be your title, which is bishop. This is what you have been made, not what you were born" (*On Consideration*, Bk. II - 17).

We really do not have to retire to a desert to imitate

the monks in their reduction of life to essentials. If we keep before our eyes who we are at birth, our essential nature as created in God's image, yet sinners, we will never need a desert to keep away everything that distracts us from God. Bernard advises the pope:

> You should be attentive not only to what you were born but also to what sort of person you are at birth, if you do not want to be cheated of the fruit and utility of your consideration. Therefore, take off these garments which you have inherited and which have been cursed from the beginning. Tear off the covering of leaves which hides your shame but does not heal your wound...candidly consider your nakedness, for you came forth naked from your mother's womb. Were you born wearing this miter? Were you born glittering with jewels or florid silk, or crowned with feathers or covered with precious metals? If you scatter all these things...you will catch sight of a naked man who is poor, wretched and miserable. A man grieving because he is man (De Con. Bk II 17-18).

The ultimate cause of all the misery in the world and in our personal life is sin. To believe this calls for an act of faith. We do have immediate knowledge that something is radically wrong in the world. We do not have immediate knowledge of the ultimate cause of the wrongness. There are, of course, many secondary causes which need attention but a true healing of the human condition has to begin deep in our hearts and spread from there like the ripples in a pond to the far shores of our life. We will never look for healing and grace unless we acknowledge our woundedness. This is true self-knowledge. Again Bernard tells the pope:

> Look at yourself closely and see if there is anything which ought to displease you....you walk more cautiously among the good if your bad points do not lie hidden. Therefore as I said, know yourself, so that in the midst of present difficulties you may draw comfort from a good conscience but even more so that you may know your deficiencies. For who is not deficient? They are totally deficient who think they in no way are deficient (Bk II - 14).

Our model in this is Jesus, who took our sinful condition upon himself. He in a sense is the prodigal son who went a long way from the Father, took the form of a swineherd slave but then shows us the way back to the Father. Unless we have, like the prodigal, an acute awareness of our state of estrangement and separation from God, we can never begin the journey to our true identity as a Divine Image in the Son.

What we begin, perhaps in fear and trembling, we are meant to end in love. The fathers who taught the way of "apatheia" or integration set out to restructure our disorganized nature under the guiding principle of love. Our hearts are made to love. Once we can free our hearts of false love and establish the love that comes from God, everything else will fall into place.

Brendan J. Freeman

We have found our anchor, or the taproot of our being. We will never come to this point, however, if we deny our sinfulness—if we never "bring a mirror and look at a dirty face" (St. Bernard De Consideration). We have to own ourselves honestly and not run from our shadow side. When we own and acknowledge our sin then we can let God's mercy into our life. We will realize we live not by our own strength because we are powerless to forgive sin—"only God can forgive sin"—but by God's mercy.

To live by God's mercy—the psalmist prayed: "When I think I am losing my foothold, your mercy Lord holds me up" (Ps. 93:18). Honestly facing ourselves and trusting in God is a life-long process and at times has the feeling of losing whatever foothold we have on life, and falling into empty space. But the mercy of God is always there to hold us up. This situation of receiving life through mercy makes us vulnerable and sensitive to others. Because we live as a gift of another, we are moved to have mercy and compassion on our neighbor who shares the same human condition.

Self-knowledge based on faith comes from seeing things as they really are. Hugh of St. Victor calls this seeing of faith contemplation: "Contemplation is an easy and clear-sighted penetration of the soul into that which is seen." This definition has a wide application.

The Pure of Heart

Thomas Merton called Albert Einstein's theory of relativity an act of contemplation. Einstein penetrated into what was before his eyes. Others had looked at the same objective reality but only Einstein penetrated into the fuller truth and meaning of what was there. Science was his basic approach to life. Faith is ours. A contemplative in our sense would be one who penetrates into reality and sees the Divine presence in it. God is present but absent from our view. We possess a divine image but we do not experience what that means. What we do experience is the absence. If we penetrate deeply into the absence we find the cause is sin. We will never find our true center—our heart—if we do not name what is so plainly before our eyes: sin, the ultimate cause of our unhappiness.

The promise to those who desire God with all their heart and who acknowledge their sin with repentance and compassion is that they will see God. This seeing can be considered the third awakening of our heart. The first awakening came when we named the cause of our restlessness as the deep center of our personal life longing for God. The second awakening came when we named the reason for our estrangement from our own center as sin and so began to listen to the call of conversion as a return to our true home in God. Now the third awakening comes when we enter into the night of faith, the absence of God, and with new eyes see God.

Brendan J. Freeman

St. Bernard, commenting on the sixth beatitude, says, "We see God face to face not only in the life to come but also in this present life, although through a glass in a dark mirror" (First Sermon for All Saints). We stood before this mirror twice before and saw with clarity that our hearts are made in the Divine Image, and that sin keeps us from possessing what we already have. Now we stand before it again but the mirror hides as much as it reveals. Through a dark mirror we catch glimmers of the vision of God, we have intimations of the Divine Presence within us. Jesus is that mirror—his humanity both reveals and hides the Glory of God.

There are only a few places in the gospels where Jesus allows his Divine nature to break through the human and reveal itself. One such case was the Transfiguration. Like the discourse on the beatitudes, the Transfiguration takes place on a mountain. There must be some significance in Jesus' choice of mountains for his important revelations. On a mountain one can see for great distances. Nothing blocks our vision of the horizon. Did you ever notice how still you become when from a high place your eyes rest on the distant horizon? Your eyes are at rest but something is tugging at your heart pulling it into eternity. St. Therese of Lisieux once said, "heart can feel what eye has never seen." The words of Jesus expand our horizon and give us a vision into eternity. They awaken our heart and we begin to feel what our eyes cannot see.

The Pure of Heart

In the event of the Transfiguration we have a paradigmatic story of how our eyes rest while our heart comes alive. When Jesus was transfigured before Peter, James and John, Peter impulsively cried out in delight, "this is wonderful, let me build three tents here...." Luke tells us he did not realize what he was saying. Peter wanted to make the moment last forever. (Or perhaps his wanting to start a building project was good preparation for becoming the first Bishop of Rome.) But Peter's response to fix the moment was not what Jesus intended for this mysterious event. We get the distinct impression the disciples were missing the meaning of what was taking place before their very eyes. Their eyes saw but their hearts did not understand. They were asleep at heart. It is only when a cloud overshadowed them and a voice spoke from the cloud do we get a sense that something deeper was taking place in the disciples.

Confronted with a great mystery they fell silent. In fact we read they were heavy with sleep. There is a beautiful Russian icon that shows Christ radiant with light and the three disciples stretched out on the ground before him fast asleep! It seems to me the cloud and the sleeping disciples signifies a deeper level of mystery. On a superficial level their senses were asleep but at a deeper level their hearts were being touched. In the darkness of the cloud a Word came to them as real and mysterious as the Word that came down from heaven when a "profound stillness encompassed everything'' (Wis.) and became flesh of the Virgin Mary.

The Word of the Father came to the disciples on the mountain and their hearts felt what their eyes could not see. The event of the Transfiguration needed the Word from heaven to give it meaning in the hearts of the disciples. The events of our life also need a word from the Father to give them meaning. Every word of the scripture is a voice from heaven for us. The message is the same; "This is my beloved Son, listen to him." Present in every situation of our life is the beloved Son. We cannot live on the level of senses only, we have to let them sleep while we enter the night of faith and there our heart awakens to something our eyes cannot see. We lose our sight to gain a vision. The awakening of our heart at this level of our being produces what the spiritual masters call "the spiritual senses of the soul."

They speak of hearing with the ears of the heart, of seeing with the eye of the soul. At baptism our external senses are anointed as a sign of the awakening of the inner senses of the spirit. Salt is put on our tongue to purify the inner sense that we may "taste Christ"—our ears are opened that we may hear the Word in our soul and a lighted candle is placed before our eyes that we may perceive with the eye of our heart the presence of Christ in every event of our journey through life.

The Pure of Heart

Seeing God can be understood as a composite of all our spiritual senses. It means to be totally immersed in God. United fully with the one in whose image we are made. But is it true, as Bernard said, that we see God in this life in some dark fashion? What does it mean to "see" God in this life? An incident from the life of St. Therese of Lisieux may help us here.

One evening Therese was helping the elderly and rather cranky Sister Peter from the church to the community dining room. There was nothing extraordinary about what she was doing, she called it an act of "charitable drudgery," but as she was helping Sister Peter her heart was awakened to a level of faith beyond description. She describes the event:

> A winter evening when I was doing my bit as usual the cold—the darkness....all of a sudden I heard far away, lovely music being played. And I constructed a picture in my imagination of a drawing room splendidly lit up, with gilded furniture; of young, fashionably dressed girls exchanging compliments and the polite small talk of society. Then I looked back at the poor invalid I was helping along. There was no music here, only a piteous groan every now and then, there was no gilding, only the plain brick of the bare convent walls faintly visible in the flickering light. Of the inner experience I had, I can tell you nothing; I only know that God enlightened my soul with rays of truth, which so outshone the tawdry brilliance of our earthly festivities as to fill me with unbelievable hap-

Brendan J. Freeman

piness. I tell you that I wouldn't have exchanged those ten minutes of charitable drudgery for a thousand years of worldly enjoyment *(Story of a Soul, p. 292).*

We see in this story how Therese was tempted, as we all are, not to be present to her life. She was trying to modify the drudgery of the moment by letting her mind wander to the realm of the unreal—the unattainable world of high society, of glitter and fashion. But through an inner experience, an awakening of her heart, a truth entered her soul and with the eye of her soul she saw what was really happening. Somehow she realized that by helping another human being she was touching God. She was "seeing" God. She had, no doubt, helped this Sister many times before and nothing happened, yet this one time truth enlightened her soul and what was always present but hidden was revealed. In the parable of the "sheep and the goats" our Lord is asked by those who were in heaven, "Lord when did we see you" and he told them all the various times they helped another human being in need they were really helping, "seeing," him.

St. Benedict begins his teaching on humility by telling his monks to "shun forgetfulness." If we are ever to see God it will only be if we are rooted firmly in reality and not living in fantasy. Benedict grounds his ladder of humility firmly in the real. We have to guard our hearts from all manner of illusion and distractions

The Pure of Heart

that takes us away from our center. When we learn how to dwell with our real life situations—the drudgery of everyday life that can be as cold and dark as a 19th century Carmelite cloister, then truth can enter our lives and let our hearts feel what our eye cannot see.

To the pure of heart all life is a mirror. If we look deeply into this mirror of life we will see the reflection of God streaming into our hearts, for we are his image. At the source of our being his life is flowing into ours. He has left his impression everywhere—in all the joys and sorrows, all the delights and disappointments of life. There is always something more than we can comprehend. The pure of heart experience that other dimension with a "clearsighted penetration of the soul into that which is seen."

The Peacemakers

Thomas Cornell

Monica: Who was that on the phone?
Tom: Margaret Garvey. She's editing a book on the beatitudes.
Monica: What does she want?
Tom: From me a chapter on "Blessed are the peacemakers."
Monica: What does she want you to do?
Tom: I guess she wants me to tell about my life as a peacemaker and how blessed I am.

IT'S presumptuous to call oneself a peacemaker, especially if it's just because one has spent the better part of one's life as a pacifist-activist. How much peace have I made? It is in the quality of inter-personal relations that one makes peace and a general of the army might do better at it than someone who goes about with a picket sign on his front and another on his back, writing and handing out denunciations of the arms race and the Administration's policies in Central America, climbing on nuclear submarines, burning draft cards, sitting in prison for the sake of international peace or for voting rights for Blacks. With that demurrer aside,

135

Thomas Cornell

I want to tell what it has been like to spend thirty-five years in the nonviolent movement for peace and social change and to give a glimpse of a kind of blessedness.

Monica and I are Catholic Workers. She was born in the movement. I came to it at age nineteen. We met, when my activist career was already in full-swing, at the Catholic Worker center in the Bowery section of New York City. I was managing editor of the monthly paper, *The Catholic Worker.* She cooked and helped with the distribution of clothing. We married, moved on to pursue the work in different ways and are still at it.

Well even before I encountered the Catholic Worker movement I had formed some unsettling questions in my mind, like "Under what circumstances, if any, am I prepared to take another human life?" And "What if the British won the war of 1776—Would George Washington's portrait hang over Miss Walsh's desk in eighth grade history class or Benedict Arnold's?" I asked Miss Walsh and her answer was a withering put-down. It seems odd that I hadn't asked myself the question, "Under what circumstances, if any, am I willing to lend myself to an institution whose purpose it is to kill massive numbers of people for political purposes, that is , the army?" Not until I was directly challenged by others who had answered that question for themselves did I entertain it for myself. The answer was: under no circumstances. To arrive at that conclusion I used a method implicit in the Catholic Worker

The Peacemakers

way of looking at things, which later became explicit in the method of liberation theology. I considered the reality of the world we live in.

Number one reality is the threat of nuclear annihilation, the destruction of civilization and all its moral and spiritual values at very least. Every war and every act of war has to be judged in the shadow of this reality. I looked at the phenomenon of war itself. World War II is a living memory for me, even if I was only a child. I remember Pearl Harbor. I had friends and cousins fighting in North Africa, Europe, the Pacific Islands. I remember how we followed specific island battles on the playground at school. I remember Hiroshima and the block-party we threw in jubilation that God had blessed our country with such power. I remember Nagasaki three days later. A very few years later I came to realize that the question: "Is war of itself immoral, *malum ut sic?*" is sterile. There is no such thing as a war as such. There are only wars in particular, and no matter how justified a war may seem at its outset, no matter how noble the stated goals, war takes on a dynamic of its own, and all questions of justice in pursuit of just ends become subsumed in the mushrooming and single goal of victory. So it is not just nuclear war that seemed to me evil, but any conceivable war fought in the modern age of total war.

These realities had to be held up to the light of faith if I was to be a man of faith. I have never been able

Thomas Cornell

to understand how people can compartmentalize their lives—faith for church and Sunday morning and miracle stories for the kids, and live as if none of it mattered the rest of the week. The light of faith. That meant scripture and what I like to call the accumulated wisdom of the believing community, what theologians call Tradition. Why does it seem so bizarre to take questions like war and how we work, how we make a living, to Jesus as he preaches on the Mount? My teachers thought it bizarre, so did my family and friends and priests. But I learned, as I studied, that not everybody thought it so strange, that the early Christians refused to serve in the Roman army even at the cost of their lives, and that the Fathers, many of them, the early teachers of the church, forbade military service, refused baptism to those who would serve, inveighed against military service in the strongest terms, comparing it to whoredom. I learned of St. Francis who forbade military service even to his lay followers in the Third Order. Later I learned of the contributions to keeping an authentic Christian witness of nonviolence alive made by Protestants, Quakers and Anabaptists particularly, and experienced how what they kept alive for us has been re-incorporated into "mainstream" Christian thinking and practice.

Becoming a conscientious objector to war and to military service was painful, but that was what I had to do on the basis of holding the realities I found up to the light of faith. It meant becoming an outsider. And it meant questioning other "givens" in the culture of my up-bringing. My family and friends were scandalized. I felt very much alone, even at the Catholic Worker, because there was not one other man my age even there going through the same thing in the mid 1950's. There were older men, there were 4-F's and there were veterans who had learned better. And there was Ammon Hennacy.

Ammon was John the Baptist, long-haired when all other males wore West Point haircuts, his costume a mis-match of items from the clothing room, his teeth mostly stubs. He had been a radical socialist before World War I, and on grounds of working class solidarity had refused to register for the World War I draft, was imprisoned and spent seven months in solitary at Atlanta, naked. He had a blanket, a bucket for body wastes, and a Bible. He said he would have read the Manhattan telephone directory seven times if that was what he had, but since it was a Bible the atheist read the Bible and emerged a non-church, Tolstoyan-type Christian. On release from prison he joined a woman he had been involved with in Milwaukee and they walked. Thelma said he walked to get Atlanta out of his system. They walked across the United States. Back in Milwaukee they began a family, with two daughters, but Thelma went her separate way and Ammon continued to work at City Welfare to see his daughters through school. On the way he joined the Christian Scientists for a brief time, and the Communist Party, for a brief time. He kept something from these associations: from "Science," as he called it, an aversion to medicine, tobacco, coffee and tea. He never ate meat either. He let the roots of his teeth rot because no dentist would extract them without anaesthesia, until he found a anarchist dentist in Maine who went along with him.

"Did it hurt?"

"I teared up a bit."

From the Communists he learned not much. He was always more radical than they. But he liked many Communists personally, and detested the witch-hunts of the 1950's and helped the rest of us to see why we had to stand with them as they were persecuted. Ammon is the only man known to have refused to register for both World War I and World War II—he was still young enough to come under the legal obligation to register in 1940. The government chose to ignore him. His daughters were not independent. Ammon chose to refuse to pay for the war and for the subsequent arms race. He took day labor as a migrant crop picker so that the "revenuers" would have to come daily to his workplace if they wished to garnishee his wages, and he wrote a column for *The Catholic Worker* called, "Life at Hard Labor." By the time I came to know him he had converted to Catholicism and had settled in at the CW

The Peacemakers

headquartes as one of its most diligent workers and its most colorful character, fasting prodigiously, forty days at a time, and picketing federal buildings. It was his idea to defy the New York State compulsory air raid drills by sitting in City Hall Park while the sirens summoned law-abiders to underground shelters, the subways, and to buildings designated as shelters against a possible enemy attack by hydrogen bomb. Two dozen people sat in the Park that year, 1953. By 1960 there were thousands defying the law, and the law was dropped.

"Ammon, I'm a conscientious objector and I want to file for exemption with my draft board. I don't know how to go about it, how I should prepare myself. Will you help me?"

"Here," he said, "read my scrap book."

It was filled with clippings going back to 1917 from newspapers, how he had refused all cooperation with the Selective Service System, how he saw it as part of the war machine, and there were pamphlets he had written and hand-bills and reports of meetings he had addressed and it was all very fine but it was no help at all to me. The third time I asked for help, and the third time he handed me his scrap-book I knew I had to go it alone. But Ammon was an example and he became a dear friend. He taught me, indirectly, that there was a real need for a program to help potential conscientious objectors, so that, years later, Jim Forest and I established the first systematized and practical program to aid young men in clarifying their objections to war and guiding them through the thicket of law and regulations governing the Selective Service System. During the Vietnam war much of our time was spent counseling large numbers of C.O.'s.

From the first, the Catholic Worker movement seemed to me to have a unique validity, an authenticity that was more hoped for than realized in other elements of the church as I experienced it, and I wanted more than anything to be a part of it, and I wanted to be a leader. Dorothy Day told me to stay in college, to stick it out, and to come around when it was over. I did. But there wasn't much I could do: serve meals, bundle the paper, help Ammon picket the Customs House. He would fast much of the time he picketed so he weakened easily, I would take his picket sign and parade for him.

"For the past twenty years I have refused to pay my federal income taxes," read one of his signs I carried. I was twenty-two years old. The crushing realization dawned on me that I had a good degree but that it meant next to nothing, that I had to learn a lot more if I was to be of any real use to the movement. So I went on projects, got involved with major demonstrations against the arms race with A.J. Muste and Dave Dellinger and Bayard Rustin, with the Committee for Nonviolent Action in New London at the submarine

The Peacemakers

base and the plant where Polaris subs were being built. And in the civil rights movement in Bridgeport and Norwalk and the Danbury areas of Connecticut. I learned a lot about the philosophy and theology of and the practice of nonviolence. I got to know leaders and got to be known by them, so that when Dorothy called me to New York in 1962 she gave me responsibility for editing *The Catholic Worker*. I was twenty-eight years old and suddenly I was where I wanted to be. The first Friday Night Meeting for the Clarification of Thought that I addressed was on the necessity of a nonviolent revolution in America. A grandiose theme, somewhat naive, I suppose, but I still believe it.

Dorothy assigned me a small cold-water apartment to share with two others and a desk at the CW center and then piled a bunch of manuscripts and galley proofs on it saying, ''You're putting out the paper. I'm going to Cuba tomorrow.'' ''But I don't know anything about putting out a paper,'' I said. ''Don't worry, here's a book on proof-reading, and the printers will teach you all you have to know.'' Off she went. I read the manual and the printers taught me, and Dorothy corrected me by mail. She worked directly with me on three issues of the paper in the next two years. She traveled a great deal at that time, and I was left to do it mostly on my own. She couldn't take many of her speaking assignments either, and most of these she passed on to me as well. I learned by doing. When she

Thomas Cornell

was in New York we spent a good deal of time together and she taught me much more.

Life was extremely hard at the CW. For weeks at a time I had the experience of having not a quarter in my pocket. Breakfast was inedible. The noon meal was the same for those who came in off the streets to the soup line, about 200 people, and for the workers—a burnt soup. That too became inedible after about a week. The evening meal was a miracle of creativity. We spent about five dollars a day to feed sixty people supper. Most of the produce was begged at the wholesale markets and much of that had to be thrown out as spoiled. Portions were meager. Left-overs went into the next day's soup. Always skinny, I lost twenty pounds.

People streamed in all hours, all day, all week: neighborhood people, men and women from the Bowery a block away, visitors, readers of the paper from around the country, from India, England, Italy, France. Some were writers, poets, intellectuals: Eli Wallach and Paddy Chaevsky, Mother Teresa, Allen Ginsberg, Abbe Pierre, Brother Antoninus, James Laughlin, Norman Thomas, Paul Goodman, Elizabeth Gurley Flynn, Scott Nearing, Judith Molina and Julian Beck. Judith and Julian organized the Living Theater a few blocks away and had achieved critical acclaim for their inventive productions. They were also anarchists and pacifists who refused to take federal taxes out of their employees' salaries. The feds clamped down on them, barred the theater and tagged everything saleable in it for public auction. The company members barricaded themselves in the theater building. The feds planned to starve them out, but we went with buckets of food and they sent down ropes and withheld the seige for some time before the company quit the U.S. for Europe, an exile of several years. Before their exile it was hard to fill their small auditorium. When visitors came from Lake Wobegone to the Worker I would sometimes ask if they had anything on their schedule for the evening. Would they like to go to the theater? I would call Julian on the phone and ask if there were eight or so seats available free that night. He was always delighted because a critic might come and the fewer empty seats the better. When the company returned from Europe years later they had to rent the massive Brooklyn Academy to accommodate the crowds they drew. One of the most affecting brief portraits of Dorothy ever written is in Judith's *Memoirs,* a recollection of the month they spent together as cell-mates in the Women's House of Detention in Greenwich Village for the Civil Defense protest. How one by one, the boisterous, flamboyant prostitutes and drug-addicted women in the notorious ''House of D'' sought Dorothy out for quiet conversation, attracted by her luminous Christianity.

But life was very hard. The demands of the Bowery

men and women were constant, the level of mental health the pits. It was hard to leave the center, a centripetal force held almost all of us workers there seven days a week, all our needs for entertainment supplied, over-supplied by the lunatics, saints and egregious sinners who poured in. I put great effort in getting out, going to organizing meetings of the nonviolent protest movement that was just beginning to gather force, making sure that the CW readership knew what was developing, keeping the CW involved. Among radicals the CW always enjoyed a good reptuation, even if the rest of the world, and most of the church, thought we were a "lunatic fringe." As a representative of the CW I enjoyed instant entry into decision-making circles in the movement, and since I was taking so many of Dorothy's speaking assignments I was doing more and more travel, at least in the Northeast. As editor of the paper I could get published too, so before long I lost my anonymity. I found a blessedness in voluntary poverty, a freedom I had never known.

When Monica and I married we left the CW community. It was not the atmosphere for a new family. We moved to an apartment of our own and supported ourselves, staying very close to the CW center. The Fellowship of Reconciliation (FOR) wanted to start a Catholic affiliate for their mostly Protestant pacifist organization and tagged Jim Forest, a young CW graduate and me to do it. Thomas Merton, the Berrigans,

The Peacemakers

Gordon Zahn, Eileen Egan, Robert Hovda, James Douglass, Betty Bartelme, Alice Mayhew, Ned O'Gorman—they all pooled their Christmas card lists and we sent out a mailing: Help us to establish a Catholic Peace Fellowship to advance active nonviolence in the Catholic community. Seed money came from the FOR and from Hermene Evans and we were off. We rented a small office and work escalated rapidly.

While I was still editing the CW paper, in the summer of 1963, a Buddhist monk in Saigon immolated himself in front of a pagoda to protest the repressive tactics of the Diem regime in Vietnam. The photograph in the American press of a robed monk, sitting upright engulfed in flames was very moving and betokened a powerful movement. U.S. involvement was central to the issues. There were no U.S. ground troops but many "advisors" in Vietnam. It was not a public issue. But some thought that there should be a response. Two of us, Chris Kearns and I, picketed the only place in New York which represented the Saigon government, the apartment building where the South Vietnamese observer to the United Nations lived. The first day the two of us picketed with a sign that read, "The Catholic Worker protests U.S. involvement in Diem's repression." The second day one of us, the third day the other and so forth. I let it be known through wider peace movement channels, the Quaker network, the War Resisters League, that the CW was having a ten-day protest at the site and that everyone was urged to join us on the tenth day. They did. We had about two hundred people and captured national media attention. That was the beginning of the Vietnam war protest. The CW remained at the center of the protest movement for the rest of the war years, becoming even more controversial than ever and reaching a wider audience than it ever had theretofore.

It had been impossible to organize programs other than the works of mercy in the maelstrom of the CW center, so the Catholic Peace Fellowship, born at the Worker, a benign front in a way (though independent and part of the FOR organizationally), became the base for anti-war programming: The first need we addressed was for counseling Catholics (and other) conscientious objectors. My own lonely experience had proven the need to me. There were no written materials, so we wrote them and gained the *imprimatur* of Cardinal Spellman, taught ourselves the law, rules and regulations of the Selective Service System, basic counseling techniques (I read Carl Rogers and Abraham Maslow, whose daughter worked down the hall as A.J. Muste's secretary) and "hung out the shingle." We fast gained a reputation as experts and men came, mostly Catholics but a considerable number of Jews, too, who knew where to get the genuine article. Our success was very high. Almost all of our clients got the classification they sought.

The Peacemakers

Thich Nhat Hanh, a Buddhist scholar-activist from Saigon came into our lives almost by accident and became our Buddhist god-father, as Tom Merton was our Christian godfather. The Buddhist monk had flown from Saigon, at the request of others in the Buddhist leadership, to JFK airport and had simply telephoned the FOR headquarters hoping for a reception. He got it. The FOR executive secretary, Alfred Hassler, sent a car to fetch Nhat Hanh, heard him out in his office in Nyack, up the Hudson a few miles from the City, and invited him to move in with his family. Thich Nhat Hanh was and is a quiet, unassuming man of deep spirituality, a Zen master, respectful of other faiths and a seeker after concordances. His mission was to make known the suppression of the Buddhists, especially the newly enlivened activists of that tradition. The war was heating up. U.S. involvement would only prolong and intensify the agony and lead to a more bitter outcome than if the forces at work in that country played themselves out. We wanted a cessation of U.S. intervention, and Nhat Hanh did also.

The political prisoners of the South Vietnam regime therefore seemed a good focus for our work: first, because they were unjustly persecuted for playing the same role in their society we played in ours as religious and humanist critics; secondly, because their torture and imprisonment was by a regime of U.S. creation; and third, because their plight, if made known to a wide American public, would undermine public and congressional support of the military intervention. As we formed a program Nhat Hanh was a presence. We hid him in a small apartment near Columbia University, where he could have access to people at the university and at Union Theological Seminary and the Jewish Seminary, where Abraham Joshua Heschel taught. Every minute with Nhat Hanh was an experience of meditation because he himself was so peacefully centered. We formed a small community, intimate enough so that we learned again what we had experienced at the Catholic Worker center, that the truth we have to share can only be conveyed in small and intimate community, and the same with peace. We make peace only in small and intimate community, even as we attempt and to a degree succeed in moving large institutions and bringing about social change.

We tried to move the U.S. public and its governmental institutions by demonstrating on the grounds of the Capitol, on its steps, setting up mock tiger cages, such as were used in Vietnam to hold political prisoners in sub-human, even crippling conditions. We took turns squatting in the tiger cages as fellow demonstrators handed out leaflets, collared tourists and Congressional aides and journalists—all who would listen. We sent delegations to the Senators and members of Congress to lobby for an end to the intervention and relief for the prisoners. We took the tiger cages around the country. And we set up Meals of Reconciliation, simple gatherings usually in a church or synagogue, with ecumenical leaders and community activists. The meal itself was a ritual, with readings from Vietnamese poetry and religious literature of the great traditions, and we ate a small bowl of rice and a cup of tea as the conditions of political prisoners, who they were, the roles they played in society as writers and artists and religious spokespeople were exposed. The meals mushroomed around the country and became a primary vehicle for organizing dissent, opposition and resistance to the war.

We engaged in mass action, helping to organize the first large demonstration, the Assembly of Unrepresented Peoples in Washington. Fifteen thousand came out and about three hundred and fifty were arrested, in a dignified and thoroughly peaceful demonstration, as we attempted to enter the Capitol itself against police orders. A.J. Muste took me to Cleveland, to a gathering of what was to be the coalition against the war called the Mobilization to End the War in Vietnam. A.J. had attended a similar coalition of labor, left-radicals, academic liberals and religious leadership twice before, in the thirties for radical social change, in the forties to ameliorate the brutality of World War II, and those efforts failed. This time he succeeded. By 1968 the largest protest demonstrations ever mounted over any issue were held in Washington.

Thomas Cornell

The political prisoners and the draft were my major preoccupations even as Jim and I were involved in coalition-building at every step. The counseling went on, and our own sheltered positions became more oppressive to Jim and to me. We were not draftable.

In August, 1965, *Life* magazine ran a story on the demonstrations beginning to spread against the war. On one side of a two-page spread was a black-and-white photograph top-to-bottom of the page, about two-thirds its width, showing Chris Kearns of the Catholic Worker burning a draft card. On the other side was a full-page color photograph of the Assembly march upon the Capitol. At one point in the march from the Washington Monument to the Capitol a hostile bystander threw a bucket of red paint at the front rank of the march, bespattering Staughton Lynd, Dave Dellinger and Robert Moses Paris, a leader of the Black civil rights movement in the Deep South. Some of us from the Catholic Worker were in the second rank, and we caught some of the paint too. It looked, in the photograph, like blood, very dramatic. Members of the Congress and Senate had been enraged by the demonstration, thinking the French Revolution was about to break out in their chambers. When some of them went to the Senate barber shop and saw the photographs they sensed in Chris's action something they could address: make the burning of draft cards a felony. And so they did, without debate, in September. The

The Peacemakers

October issue of *The Catholic Worker* had a suggestion by me that the time had come to burn draft cards as a symbol of resistance. Some young men at the CW headquarters started talking about doing it. I felt a responsibility to join them, because I had burned my old draft cards, several times as a matter of fact, and had urged others to do the same. How could I withhold myself now that the penalties would be real for me? I ordered new draft cards from my draft board, and in November we burned our cards, five of us, in a well organized demonstration of about twenty-five hundred at Union Square in New York City. Dorothy spoke in our support, and A.J. There was a small group of counter-demonstrators across the street, kept away by a large contingent of New York City police. They shouted "Moscow Mary" at Dorothy, and "Burn yourselves, not your draft cards" at us. An infiltrator made the photographs of the event even more arresting when he aimed a jet of water from a fire extinguisher at us just as we attempted to ignite our cards. The cards burned anyway.

As the demonstration disbanded we were hustled away by police in squad cars. We were not placed under arrest but taken to our offices, away from the scene for our safety's sake.

The next morning, a Sunday, the photograph of the five of us and the jet of water and our burning cards was on the front page of the *New York Times*, all the other New York papers, the Connecticut papers, the English language paper in Paris and we were instant celebrities or villains. I had enjoyed a certain small fame, as I have since, and the lesson I learned from it is this: the more people know you the less they know you. That is, the farther you get from the intimate community, the less you are able to communicate, the more distorted what you communicate becomes. The less peace you are able to make. The larger the crowd the lonelier you become.

At this point tragedy intervened. One of the volunteers at the Catholic Worker, Roger LaPorte, a young man of unstable mental health who had attended the draft-card burning and who had heard the chant, "Burn yourselves, not your draft card," did just that. A few days after the demonstration, early in the morning, about five o'clock, he sat before the UN secretariat building, poured two gallons of gasoline over himself, and lit a match. A reporter friend from the *New York Post* telephoned me with the news. I got back into bed, terribly shaken. At about eight a.m. I called Dorothy, who had alread learned the news.

We knew we had to respond, to answer questions from the press, but we knew also that this would be a very dangerous business because we might unwillingly lead others to imitate Roger. An elderly Midwestern woman had burned herself to death in protest against the war. A Quaker had done the same in front of the Pentagon. Neither of us mentioned it, but I'm sure that Dorothy was as aware as I that the reputation of the Catholic Worker movement was on the line also. We didn't want to diminish Roger's sacrifice. We did not want to question it. But we wanted to steer others away from imitation. I wrote a draft release for the press, read it to Dorothy about ten a.m. on the telephone. She authorized it and told me to speak to the media. No one else was to say anything. She would write of it in her regular column in the CW later.

Our little office was a flight above the last elevator stop in an old building in the lowest part of Manhattan. Television crews had to carry heavy equipment with all their cables up the stairs and cram it all into our little warren. CBS, NBC, ABC, Canadian television, reporters from radio and the press streamed in, one after the other, all day. Murray Kempton was one of the first. He helped me to write the draft release. I was terrified of saying the wrong thing, the least shade of meaning could be fatally important. He saw how I had to leave the presence of reporters every now and then to regain my composure, so he stayed with me all through the day. The last call of the day was from Montreal television. Toward the end of the interview the reporters said, ''That's funny, the lights have gone out, it appears, all over the city.'' I said, ''The lights just went out here too.'' As Roger lay dying of his burns at Bellvue Hospital, the lights went out from

Thomas Cornell

Canada to Virginia. It was the Great Black-Out of 1965. Jim and I closed the office and walked the three or four miles back to the CW headquarters. The only light was from car head-lights. Someone had found a burnt-out box spring on the Bowery and stuck candles in the springs and suspended the grotesque candelabra from the CW ceiling. The dining area was filled with mourners. We took many of them to our nearby apartments for mutual consolation. I learned later that more than one of that group secretly considered imitating Roger. Dan Berrigan was most healing in his ministry to the young people, Roger's friends and fellow workers. There were no more self-immolations. A blessing.

Corporate resistance to the war was the goal of our banding together as five men in the act of draft card burning, and for months it seemed that our goal was not attained. But gradually the Resistance took incohate shape around the country, in New York, Chicago and Los Angeles, and draft card burnings and organized draft resistance became a fact—but by that time we were in prison, the Supreme Court having refused to hear our appeal. My daughter, our second child, took her first steps for me in the visitors' room at Danberry Federal Correctional Institution. I served five out of six months' sentence, and was lucky at that, because most draft law offenders were sentenced to from two to three years, and most men served about two years in prison.

The Peacemakers

In the most wretched conditions I ever experienced there was palpable blessedness, especially in reading St. Paul's prison letters.

Jim Forest was also in prison in 1968, in Wisconsin. He had joined thirteen others in seizing the 1-A files from the draft board in Milwaukee. The "Milwaukee 14" took the files to a square outside the Selective Service System offices and burned them publicly. They waited for the police, praying the Lord's Prayer, were arrested, tried and convicted. Jim used his time well, writing prodigiously, and resting, something he has never done well. A small blessing.

Thich Nhat Hanh had been assigned by the Buddhist leadership to go to Paris, to head an unofficial Buddhist Peace Delegation at the Paris Peace Talks. French was his second language, and he felt less out of place in France than in New York, but he suffered exile, not knowing when or if he would ever be allowed to go home. He is still in France. The new government wants him about as much as the old one did. From France he was in constant communication with the Buddhist leadership in Saigon. There a secret activist employed by the prison system purloined the files of the political prisoners and Xeroxed them, put the originals back in their files and sent a copy to Nhat Hanh. He sent the package to us in Nyack from Paris, asking that we get the information to the Vatican. Why he didn't just get on the train and take them to Rome himself I didn't

Thomas Cornell

understand, but I did as he asked. The International FOR was to meet in Holland, and I was to attend. Pax Christi International was to meet in Strasbourg, France right after. I arranged to attend that as well, brought the package of information to the International conference at the Conseil d'Europe and hoped for a hearing. A well-placed friend asked the Steering Committee for the conference to hear me. They refused. The agenda was established. No new items. I waited. On the last day of the conference the microphones were opened to the floor. I was one of the first recognized. "My name is Tom Cornell, I am program director for the Fellowship of Reconciliation in the United States and come to you from a meeting of the executive committee of the International FOR which just met in Dorn, The Netherlands. I bring with me an urgent concern of our International: that is the plight of the political prisoners of the Saigon regime in Viet Nam. I have with me . . . . " I told the story of how the information I carried was obtained, and asked that the good office of Pax Christi be used to notify the Vatican of the need to act on the issue. My French is very poor, but I understood the references by speaker after speaker to "l'intervention de Monsieur Cornell d'IFOR." As the assembly was being dismissed someone came to me and said that Cardinal Alfrink, the president of Pax Christi International, wanted to see me. Alfrink asked me to draft a wire to be sent to the Vatican over his signature for the International. He signed what I wrote and I flew to Rome.

Cardinal John Wright had helped me before, so I went immediately to him, showed him what I had and asked how do you get this sort of thing to the right desk so that it would be seen by the right people. Things have a way of getting lost in big bureaucracies, I had come to know. And even with the message from Cardinal Alfrink telling the Nunciature to expect me I wanted to make sure. Wright sent me to Cardinal Sergio Pignedoli, one of the most charming men I have ever known, who got on the telephone himself and made all the contacts necessary. At just that time President Thieu of South Vietnam was making his last bid for international legitimacy and attempted to use the Vatican for that purpose. He was scheduled to meet privately and then publicly with Pope Paul VI. The Italian Communist Party was delighted to have an occasion to rally in St. Peter's Square against the pope as a symbol of political conservatism, and a large mass of protesters was anticipated The pope turned the tables on Thieu. Whenever a microphone was open Pope Paul referred to the political prisoners. The protest rally fizzled, the pope and the church were saved an embarrassment, Thieu's purpose was frustrated and I felt a blessedness.

After the war was over and the new regime took over in Saigon, Thich Nhat Hanh wrote from France again.

Thomas Cornell

He still could not go home. Some of the same people who had been imprisoned by the old government were still in jail under the new one, especially Buddhist activists. He telephoned and urged most desperately that we use whatever small influence we might have with representatives of the new government in New York for release of the prisoners. Jim Forest and I drafted a respectful letter, gently alluding to the years we had struggled and the price many of us had paid for our efforts to get the U.S. out of Vietnam, wishing the new leadership well in its efforts for reconstruction etc. and pleading for the political prisoners. Pastor Richard John Neuhaus worked on the draft. We circulated it to as many well-known figures in the American anti-war movement as we could find in our address files and gathered over one hundred signatures to the letter. The Vietnamese representatives to the United Nations refused to receive the letter or even to open their door to Dan Berrigan, Jim and the others who tried to deliver it. So we released it to the newspapers and a new storm of controversy broke. Some of the anti-war leadership thought we were badly out of turn to make this request of the Vietnamese since it was our government that had caused the trouble in Vietnam in the first place, and that the fact that we had resisted our government gave us no standing in the matter.

A few signers withdrew their names under pressure. The press chose to interpret the story as "division in the ranks of the peace movement," with Jane Fonda on one side and Joan Baez on the other. Jane opposed us and Joan supported us. A coalition that was always fragile began to unravel. It didn't seem like any blessedness to be reviled by comrades as bitterly as by political foes.

It is not useless to attempt peacemaking through large institutions, just very difficult. When I filed as a conscientious objector in 1956 I did so as a Catholic, using arguments from classical Catholic teaching in the hope that the church would somehow, someday support me and the others who would be coming after. In 1963, Pope John XXIII made that hope more real with his encyclical *Pacem In Terris*, and then the Vatican Council, convened later that year gave explicit recognition and even praise to conscientious objectors. But the church in America was moving slowly. Only when the war was winding down did the bishops quietly condemn the war as "disproportionate," so gently that hardly anyone noticed.

When President Jimmy Carter reinstituted registration for the military draft the bishops' staff called me down to their headquarters in Washington to consult on the church's response. I was astounded at the recognition my work had won. The bishops' staff accepted my recommendations, including a statement that the office of the church should be made available for the counseling of any who are troubled by the draft. Then, in the spring of 1982, the bishops' staff called me again, to consult on the first draft of the pastoral letter on peace and disarmament. The final draft fell short of our hopes but was a great leap forward, recognizing the tradition of Christian nonviolence, citing Martin Luther King and Dorothy Day as its modern apostles, and accepting nuclear deterrence only conditionally and temporarily.

An outright condemnation of the deterrent was an unrealistic hope that some of us can never abandon. The letter opened the door to wide education on peace issues in the church and beyond it, and I was sure that had the Catholic Worker failed to keep a responsible and authentically Christian posture during those long years of war, when so many elements in the wider movement went beyond responsibility, we would not have had that letter; Christian and Catholic nonviolence would not have gained its limited credibility. A great blessedness. It had been hard to keep the newer members of the New York community within the bounds of responsibility, when they were too young to have known anything but increasing frustration at a war that kept on and on for over a decade despite all that we could do. Dorothy remembered those years as the hardest of her life. Mine too.

Another political prisoner came to our attention, one in Buenos Aires. He was the coordinator of the small FOR affiliate in Argentina called *Servicio Paz y Justicia,* and outside the tiny circle of dedicated nonviolent activists and artists at the university where he taught sculpture, hardly anyone had heard of Adolfo Perez

The Peacemakers

Esquivel, not even in his home city. People were disappearing in Argentina in those years of the "dirty war." Adolfo was lucky. He was simply interned. No charges were ever placed against him and he was never brought before a judge. But his place of imprisonment was known and his wife could visit him. She pleaded that we do something. I visited the Argentine ambassador to the United Nations, an excellent worker for the cause of disarmament and personally a decent man, but in no position to do anything but cable his government that I had made the inquiry about Adolfo, why he was in prison, and why he was not released if no charges were to be placed against him. Andrew Young was then U.S. Ambassador to the UN, and I had worked under him in Selma, Alabama during the height of the civil rights movement. "The last time I came here to the U.S. Mission to the UN, Andy, I was arrested by federal marshalls and hauled off to jail. Today I sit here with you over sandwiches and Coke." Andy told one of his aides to get on the phone to the State Department. "An old friend of Andy's is here with a request for information on a man named Adolfo Perez Esquivel. Cable the Casa Rosada in Buenos Aires and let them know that we want information on this guy." Adolfo was released soon after and the next year was awarded the Nobel Peace Prize. Neither he nor *Servicio Paz y Justicia* would be obscure again. Blessedness.

Work in the peace movement, peacemaking, has brought me to Panama, Ireland, England, Italy, Sici-

Thomas Cornell

ly, Nicaragua, Egypt, Lebanon, Syria, Jordan, Israel, Mexico, Canada and all but six or seven of the fifty States. I had worked with half a dozen Nobel Prize winners and cardinals of the church, and sometimes there has been some effect, some movement, almost always other than anticipated.

Peacemaking comes from within and is brought about face to face. This morning I will be at our soup kitchen, this afternoon with my son at our other soup kitchen. A couple of hundred men and women, and a good number of children from a violent ghetto, people who know that they are rejects of the consumerist, capitalist society around them will gather in need of food, clothing and shelter, in need of counsel, instruction and encouragement. They will see Christian symbols on the walls, they will hear a "God bless you." They will eat and be warm, for a while. Our daughter is back at her college, just returned from Nicaragua with terrible stories to tell, and stories of heroism and endurance. Monica will keep our house of hospitality running almost smoothly.

Our children are among the first of the third biological generation of Catholic Workers. They are peacemakers. Our Catholic Worker network of houses and communal farms is larger than it has ever been, over one hundred around the country. The majority of Workers are too young to have known Peter or Dorothy but they give promise of a future for our movement. These are the blessings, the blessedness we enjoy.

The Persecuted

Julia Loesch

"Kindness and Truth will meet,
Justice and Peace will kiss:
Truth springs up from the earth,
And Justice reaches down from heaven."

Psalm 85:10-11

L IKE the dancing of paralytics and the clear sight of the eyeless blind, the "meeting" of Kindness and Truth, Justice and Peace, is one of the wonders of the Messianic Age. It seems miraculous that these particular virtues could coexist.

We all know people who pride themselves on being "brutally honest," but who seem to take more pleasure in the brutality than in the honesty. We admire *truth*, of course, but there are truthtellers any of us would cross a county to avoid.

On the one hand, there are "kind" people who would let an untruth slide indefinitely if challenging it would make somebody seriously uneasy. ("Feel" and "comfortable" are big words with them: "How

165

do you feel about this decision?'' ''I'm comfortable with it.'')

In the same way there are peace advocates who will pretty-please pacify things even if the hostages' throats are being slit, elsewhere, while the peace party's going on; and justice advocates who will have their Justice, by God, even if they have to destroy the earth itself in the process.

We also know compromise: truth-on-Monday and kindness-by-Thursday; a little-bit-of-justice balanced with the right-amount-of-peace. But to find somebody who lives *TruthKindness* and *JusticePeace,* full strength, flaming hot, and fused like bronze: this would be a sign of the Messianic Age. Such a person is a Soldier of the Lamb.

* * * *

I first met Joan Andrews in 1985 in Pittsburgh, Pennsylvania, when, along with about a dozen other people, we were arrested for blocking the door of an abortion clinic.

I'd heard a few things about her, formidable things. Joan's done 100 sit-ins, ''rescues,'' ''actions,'' they said. Maybe 150. Joan never cooperates with the cops, they said. She doesn't play ball. She fasts in jail.

I thought: spare me! Grim. A Fanatic. You can admire that kind of person from afar but you probably wouldn't want to spend a weekend with her.

The Persecuted

The activists had a brief planning meeting at a Burger King about a block and a half from our target. Women's Health Services is the Abortion Pentagon of the tri-state area: about 10,000 women come into this place every year for "the procedure." When they walk in, they have babies. When they walk out, they don't. Even from the standpoint of sanitary disposal, it boggles the mind. One would expect to see the Allegheny River running red.

Joan, a plain-faced, poorly-dressed woman—37 at that time—said nothing at this tactical meeting. I didn't hear a peep from her during the two hours when we were blocking the doors to the "Procedure Rooms." I can't tell you whether she sang or prayed aloud, as most of us did, or if she spoke to the clinic personnel, the teenagers waiting for abortions, or the police. And when we were hauled off the premises and ended up at the police lock-up I lost sight of her altogether.

After ten hours' wait, I was, I thought, the last one to be called out for the bond hearing in front of the magistrate. All the other women were released on their own recognizance.

"Since you're from out-of-county," I heard the magistrate say, "we are imposing a $100 cash bond."

"I—haven't got it."

"Then you are remanded to the custody of the County. Matron, take her back to her cell."

When a whole group is being jailed, there's a wonderful *esprit de corps*, but now I was alone.

167

Julia Loesch

To my humiliation, I recognized the onset of my old claustrophobic terror. My heart pounded; I broke out in sweat; I experienced a choking, suffocating sensation. I had the insane desire—and if you've never experienced a phobia, you won't know what to make of this—to tear off my clothes and batter myself against the bars.

The Matron peered in at me. "You're really in distress, aren't you, honey? I'll put you over here with your girlfriend." And she transfered me into the cell with Joan Andrews.

Now I felt a wretched shame. What did I expect this formidable woman to say? (You haven't even spent one night in jail! Get a grip!)

"Joan," I said, "I'm sorry. I feel so weird."

She sat down next to me and put an arm around me. "You're shaking. You feel like jumping out of your skin. I know."

Taking both my hands she began a Rosary—as I realized a few Sorrowful Mysteries later, when I was calm enough to understand the words.

"Are you thirsty?" she asked me. "Here, take this." She handed me a half-pint of milk and a sandwich: her portion of the lunch the rest of us had wolfed down five hours before.

"Didn't you eat?" I asked.

After some prodding, she admitted she was fasting.

I wanted very much to keep her talking. I kept asking her questions about her life. Joan answered.

The Persecuted

She grew up in rural Tennessee, south of Nashville, Her mother, Betty, is a registered nurse. Her father, William, has a law degree, but he didn't like arguing ("*Imagine* such a lawyer!" she laughed) so they all settled down to something they liked better: farming.

She and her three brothers and two sisters were all born at home. When Joan was about nine, she remembered, her mother had a miscarriage. The children all were shown their tiny brother's delicate body. Into the box which was lovingly made for his burial, each of the children placed a lock of hair.

"I was so sad," she said. "I thought, that could have been me when I was a baby. But I knew that God had taken my little brother to heaven."

At the age of 12, Joan saw a young cousin of hers struggling in a swift, rocky stream near the family picnic site. Joan couldn't swim, but she jumped in the water and tried to reach the cousin.

"Did you save him?"

"God is so good. The current carried us both to the other shore."

"Weren't you scared?"

"I was afraid of drowning. But I was more afraid of doing nothing."

"Do you miss farm life and your family?"

"Oo-o-h." A seven-syllable sigh. "My two favorite things—when I'm not saving babies—are horses—and—matchmaking!" She shot me a glance and laughed. I suddenly noticed how pretty she was.

Julia Loesch

"Do you want to get marrried? And have kids?"
Yes, she did.
"Do you have somebody special?"
Sadness. No. Not exactly. There was a man she cared
for, but he wanted her not to "rescue babies" anymore.
"Do *you* have somebody special?" she asked.
"Aah—. Sort of. No."
Her face grew bright with merriment. "Specify. What
kind of guy are you looking for?"
"Are you serious?" I laughed.
"I've already matched up ten friends—five couples—
and I'd love to do the same for you."
By this time, we were both giggling like 15-year-olds.
We were helpless with silliness, when the Matron came
to the cell door with an announcement: "Miss Loesch?
You can go now. Your buddies outside have raised
your bond."
"But I don't *want* to go," I gasped.
"You go," said Joan, seriously. "You're not ready
to refuse bond. Maybe you will be some day, but not
now." And without a hint of reproach—or any reference to the fact that I was leaving her alone in the cell
for God knows how long—she sent me on my way.

* * * *

Joan Andrews' first arrest was in Nashville in the
early 60's, when she joined with other young high-
school students, black and white, in integrating a racial-

ly segregated lunch-counter. Her mother recalls that she "wanted to be treated just like the black children." Her attitude was: *If you serve me, serve them. If you reject them, reject me. We're together.*

She attended St. Louis University, and was briefly affiliated with the anti-Vietnam War movement.

"People opposed the violence of the war in Vietnam, the killing there, because they were humanitarians," she once told an interviewer. "And many, because they were Christians, believed in God and believed in the love of your neighbor and your enemy." But she became disappointed with much of what she saw of the anti-war movement.

"There were so many sins against purity," she explained briefly.

By the late 60's, Joan sensed that what began in impurity would end up in violence against anyone who was smaller and weaker: men against women, women against children.

In 1973, the Supreme Court's Roe vs Wade decision struck down the laws in all 50 states which had protected the lives of children during their prenatal development. Joan and her sisters went down to the abortion sites and stood on the sidewalks hour after hour, day after day, asking girls, women, couples, not to destroy what God had begun in them. They offered shelter to women with crisis pregnancies. They did educational work. They lobbied.

By the late 70's, Joan had found a way to identify

even more profoundly with the endangered unborn child. She decided to join the sit-ins being organized by the Pro-Life Action League in nearby Missouri. Like others in the movement, Joan was arrested 30, 40, 50 times or more in St. Louis alone.

Why did she do it?

Partly as a last-ditch attempt to appeal to the aborting mothers. She knew from experience that they were often ambivalent enough about their abortion decision to respond positively to an eleventh-hour plea.

"If you save one mom and her baby, you don't mind the sacrifice [of imprisonment]," she told a reporter from a college newspaper. "Just look what Jesus gave to save our lives!"

But in Joan's heart, there was always the sense of *being with*, even of standing *in the place of*, the endangered person.

That has become a rationale for her non-cooperation in court. The unborn have no voice, no lawyer, no right of appeal, and neither will she.

* * * *

Joan was arrested many times without being convicted (this was common in the early days of the pro-life direct action movement in St. Louis), and then served numerous short sentences in local jails across America. She simply entered abortion facilities, talked

The Persecuted

to the women, blocked doorways, and (when, rarely, she had the chance) attempted to disassemble the suction abortion machines.

She had baby-pictures sent to her by young mothers, grateful because she stood between them and the abortionist long enough for them to change their minds. She had notes from women like "D.S." thanking her for "working with zeal to help me get on my feet and be able to support the life I, with your urging, had decided to spare."

And she was never convicted of much more than trespassing—until Pensacola.

* * * *

Several abortion facilities had been bombed in Pensacola, Florida, in late 1984. The clinics were empty and nobody was endangered or injured. But when two young couples were arrested for the bombings, the extended public drama of their trial and conviction had a chilling effect on the whole pro life movement in Pensacola.

"It's like, people were spooked," said one local activist. "They didn't want to do *anything*. No picketing, no sidewalk-counseling. People were afraid that if they even wrote a letter to the editor against abortion, their neighbors would say, 'Are you one of those bombers?' "

Julia Loesch

Joan could sympathize with the defendants' goal of "actually stopping abortions and not just talking about it." But she was deeply concerned to show the world that you can "actually stop abortions" through non-violent actions.

On March 26, 1986, after having informed the police and the abortion staffers of her intentions, Joan Andrews entered an empty, unoccupied procedure room at the Ladies' Center, an abortion site in the city of Pensacola, and attempted to unplug the electrical cord on the suction abortion machine. She was immediately seized by the police, who were on site waiting for her.

Six months later—having spent the entire pre-trial period in prison—she was convicted of resisting arrest without violence, and burglary (which in Florida law involves entering onto private property).

The prosecutor, pointing out her previous record, asked the judge to impose what he considered to be a very stiff sentence: one year imprisonment. But when Judge William Anderson began to outline conditions for possible probation, Joan made it clear that she did not consider unplugging a suction machine to be a crime.

"As a matter of conscience, I cannot accept probation, community control or restitution, or pay a fine. I can only be put in jail or released. Anything else [involves] an agreement to let human beings be killed."

The Persecuted

Judge Anderson gave Joan Andrews a five-year prison term.

* * * *

After receiving the sentence, Joan told the court, "The only way I can protest for unborn children now is by non-cooperation in jail."

With that, she dropped to the floor, sat cross-legged before the judge, and refused to move.

Shackled hand and foot, she was shortly thereafter driven in a van for 600 miles to Lowell State Prison where, because of her non-cooperation, she was put in solitary confinement.

"I've been very blessed to have been able to keep my rosary and my St. Alphonsus Stations of the Cross," said Joan in a letter to friends on the outside. "I figure this can be a temporary, five-year stay in the cloister. A little convent is good for everybody."

Attempts to have her certified insane failed because the resident psychiatrists at Lowell insisted she was a woman of conviction. Because she refused to sign any papers which implied in any way that she was guilty of a "crime" or in need of "rehabiliation," she was transferred again—to Florida's maximum security Broward Correctional Institution.

"When I informed the Reception and Orientation

sergeant that I could not cooperate, things got a little ruffled for awhile," she wrote a few weeks later, adding, "The lieutenant in charge gave me a tour of the confinement wing to scare me into changing my mind."

A devout Catholic, Joan was denied the right to attend Mass. A Tennessee farmer, she was denied the sight of meadows, sun and sky.

In a July, 1987, letter to a friend, Joan described the sounds and sights of violence which she could continuously hear and, sometimes, see from her confinement cell: fights between prisoners, suicide attempts. She said that some inmates egg each other on to kill themselves or to assault prison personnel, "while others call out for her not to harm herself. Then there is cursing between the two factions as they show their hatred for each other."

And later: "I do think the judges and prosecutors know what they're doing when the send us to these places. They're not doing it simply to protect 'decent' society from us nasty pro-life rescuers—they put us here to torture us. They know what we face here. It's like one long, endless rape." But she added that "I still feel amazing comfort from our good God."

Warden Marta Villacorta believes Joan Andrews is not a criminal and should not be in prison—certainly not in Broward, which houses women convicted of violent crimes and who are considered too dangerous to hold in other facilities.

The Persecuted

"[Andrews is] in disciplinary now because she refuses to answer questions, fill out forms, be part of the prison community," Villacorta told newspaper reporters. "The other prisons are for people who cooperate."

* * * *

The closer we are to the preborn children, the more faithful we are, the more closely we become identified with them. This is our aim. This is our goal. To wipe out the line of distinction between the preborn and their born friends, becoming ourselves discriminated against. . . . Why should we be treated differently?

The rougher it gets for us, the more we can rejoice that we are succeeding. No longer are we being treated so much as the privileged born but as the discriminated-against preborn. I don't want to be treated any differently than my brother, my sister. You reject him, you reject me. . .

We do not expect justice in the courts. Furthermore, we do not seek it for ourselves when it is being denied our beloved preborn brothers and sisters. The true defendants [the unborn children] were killed without due process on the day of the rescue attempt. We only stand here in their stead, being substitute defendants by a compelling and painful logic.

They died for the crime of being preborn and unwanted. We expect no justice from a judicial system which decrees such savagery and a government which allows it. If it is a crime punishable by death to be unwanted, maybe it should be a crime, punishable by death, to love the unwanted and to act to protect them.

Would that I could crawl back into that violated sanctuary of the womb, and be them. But Jesus already did that—and Jesus will forever be the preborn Christ Child because the Redemp-

tive Act of the Incarnation, the human and divine conception of Jesus, is at all times present.

Victory in this struggle to end the holocaust is not going to be easy, nor pain-free, but we can and must always have great joy in our hearts and souls. And the victory to come will probably not be soon. I am sure there will be much suffering first. But, oh, thank God, we have finally realized this and are all of us taking up the Cross we must each help to bear.

I see our people letting go more and more, growing spiritually, growing deeper and deeper in love with God, with each other, with the precious babies—and in a very real and heart-thrillingly holy way, more and more loving those who engineer, perpetrate, and commit the holocaust. With true love for them. . . .

The best thing anyone can do for me is just what you have been doing: going out and protecting God's precious children as the Lord leads you.

God bless you and Mary keep you in her care.

Joan Elizabeth Andrews

* * * *

It was the simplest, most normal response to a machine dangerous to nearby children: pull out the plug. Does Joan Andrews repent of doing it? No. Would she promise never to do it again? No.

Because of her refusal of any release conditions, and in the absence of a pardon from Florida's Governor Robert Martinez, it now appears that Joan Andrews will serve five years in prison for this action. As long

The Persecuted

as she refuses to sign papers, "play the game," or accept the label or role of "convicted criminal," she will probably serve out this sentence in solitary confinement.

Happy are those who are persecuted for the cause of right. Theirs is the kingdom of heaven.

Contributors

Audacity to Believe is SHEILA CASSIDY's account of her life in Chile from 1971-75, during which time she was imprisoned and tortured. She is a physician at a hospice for the dying in Plymouth, England, and a contributor to *The Tablet* of London.

THOMAS CORNELL is a founder of the Catholic Peace Fellowship and Pax Christi USA. He serves as a deacon in the diocese of Waterbury, Conn. and, with his wife, Monica, directs Guadalupe House of Hospitality.

Father BRENDAN J. FREEMAN recently celebrated his 30th anniversary as a Trappist. He has served as Abbot of Our Lady of New Melleray, Dubuque, Iowa, for five years.

Wife and mother of three, MARGARET QUIGLEY GARVEY is currently working with severely mentally retarded in South Bend, Indiana. In 1973 she began a Catholic Worker House of Hospitality in Davenport, Iowa where she resided for seven years. She co-edited *The Dorothy Day Book* with her husband, Michael. She has also worked in Campus Ministry at the University of Notre Dame and Western Illinois University.

Contributors

PATRICK JORDAN is an editor of *Commonweal* and a past editor of *The Catholic Worker*. He has worked at St. Rose's Home, a small hospital for terminal cancer patients operated by the Hawthorne Dominicans in New York City.

RACHELLE LINNER has been part of the Community for Creative Non-Violence in Washington, D.C., the Alderson Hospitality House in Alderson, West Virginia. A resident of Boston, her free-lance writing has focused on Hiroshima since she spent a month there in 1984.

Currently serving a year's probation sentence for her activities in the pro-life movement JULIA LOESCH is a contributing editor for the *New Oxford Review* and a frequent contributor to the *National Catholic Register*.

BRIAN MICLOT, a priest of the Davenport, Iowa Diocese, is presently doing graduate work in philosophy at the University of Notre Dame. He studied for the priesthood at St. John's, Collegeville, and served nine years in urban and rural ministries in southeast Iowa. While completing his doctoral studies he is developing a ministry to "those on the fringes," the people of the streets in South Bend.

Contributors

In addition to her position as professor of religious studies at St. Mary's College, BONITA RAINE is Director of Adult Programs at Logan in South Bend, Ind.— an organization providing services for the mentally retarded. She served as legal guardian for the young man she writes about in these pages.